SCALABLE DATA PIPELINES

ARCHITECTING FOR THE PETABYTE ERA

Oreoluwa Adebayo

DEDICATION

This book is dedicated to the countless data engineers and architects who work tirelessly behind the scenes to build and maintain the invisible infrastructure that powers our data-driven world. Your dedication to reliability, scalability, and efficiency often goes unnoticed, but your contributions are fundamental to the progress of science, business, and society. It is also dedicated to my family, whose unwavering support and encouragement made this endeavor possible. Your patience and understanding during the long hours of writing were a constant source of motivation.

Finally, this book is for the aspiring data professionals who are embarking on their journey to master the art of building scalable data pipelines. May this book serve as a guiding light in your exploration of the petabyte era.

TABLE OF CONTENTS

FOREWORD

It is with great pleasure that I write the foreword for Oreoluwa Adebayo's timely and insightful book, "Scalable Data Pipelines: Architecting for the Petabyte Era." In today's data-saturated world, the ability to effectively manage and process vast amounts of information is no longer a luxury but a fundamental necessity for any organization seeking to thrive.

Oreoluwa, through his extensive experience and deep understanding of the data landscape, has crafted a comprehensive guide that tackles the critical challenges of building data pipelines at scale. This book goes beyond theoretical concepts and delves into the practical considerations and architectural patterns that are essential for navigating the complexities of the petabyte era.

The insights shared within these pages are not just relevant for today's challenges but also provide a solid foundation for building data infrastructure that can adapt to the evolving demands of tomorrow. Whether you are a seasoned data engineer, a budding data architect, or a technology leader grappling with the realities of big data, this book offers invaluable guidance and practical strategies.

Oreoluwa Adebayo's passion for the field and his commitment to sharing knowledge are evident throughout the book. He has successfully distilled complex concepts into accessible language, making this a valuable resource for a wide audience.

I highly recommend "Scalable Data Pipelines: Architecting for the Petabyte Era" to anyone who is serious about harnessing the power of data on a scale. It is a must-read for those who are building the data infrastructure of the future.

PREFACE

The digital landscape is being reshaped at an unprecedented pace, driven by an exponential surge in data generation. From the mundane clicks of online interactions to the complex sensor readings of industrial IoT devices, data is no longer a trickle but a torrential downpour. This deluge presents both immense opportunities and significant challenges. Organizations that can effectively harness, process, and analyze this vast ocean of information stand to gain invaluable insights, drive innovation, and achieve a competitive edge. However, the traditional approaches to data management and processing often falter when confronted with the sheer volume, velocity, and variety of data in the petabyte era.

This book, "Scalable Data Pipelines: Architecting for the Petabyte Era," is born out of the necessity to navigate this new data reality. It is a guide for data engineers, architects, scientists, and anyone involved in building and maintaining robust and scalable data infrastructure. We delve into the core principles, architectural patterns, and practical techniques required to design and implement data pipelines that can not only handle today's massive datasets but are also future proofed for the even greater data volumes to come.

Within these pages, you will find a comprehensive exploration of the key considerations for building scalable data pipelines, from data ingestion and storage to transformation, processing, and delivery. We will examine various technologies and frameworks, discuss best practices for performance optimization and fault tolerance, and explore the evolving landscape of cloud-based data solutions.

This book is not just about theoretical concepts; it is grounded in practical experience and real-world challenges. It aims to equip you with the knowledge and tools necessary to architect data pipelines that are not only scalable but also reliable, efficient, and adaptable to the ever-changing demands of the petabyte era. Join us on this journey to unlock the power of big data through the art and science of scalable data pipelines.

INTRODUCTION

The petabyte era is no longer a futuristic concept; it is the present reality for many organizations. The sheer scale of data being generated daily necessitates a fundamental shift in how we approach data management and processing. Traditional batch-oriented systems and monolithic architectures often struggle to cope with the velocity and volume of modern datasets. This is where the concept of scalable data pipelines becomes critical.

A data pipeline is a series of interconnected steps that transform raw data into usable information. In the petabyte era, these pipelines must be designed with scalability as a core principle. They need to be able to handle massive data volumes, process them efficiently, and adapt to fluctuating data loads without compromising performance or reliability.

This book provides a comprehensive guide to architecting such scalable data pipelines. We will explore the fundamental building blocks of a modern data pipeline, including data ingestion techniques for efficiently and reliably bringing data from various sources into the pipeline; scalable and cost-effective data storage solutions capable of handling petabyte-scale datasets; data transformation methods for cleaning, shaping, and preparing data for analysis at scale; data processing using distributed computing frameworks and techniques for processing massive datasets in parallel; data delivery strategies for making processed data accessible to downstream systems and users; and monitoring and management tools and techniques for ensuring the health, performance, and reliability of data pipelines.

We will also delve into key architectural patterns for building scalable systems, such as distributed computing, microservices, and cloud-native architectures. We will examine various technologies and frameworks commonly used in the big data ecosystem, including but not limited to Apache Spark, Apache Kafka, cloud-based data warehousing solutions, and serverless computing.

This book is intended for a broad audience, including data engineers looking to deepen their understanding of scalable architectures, data architects responsible for designing robust data infrastructure, data scientists seeking to optimize their data processing workflows, and technology leaders aiming to leverage the power of big data within their organizations. While some familiarity with data processing concepts will be beneficial, we will strive to explain complex topics in a clear and accessible manner.

Our goal is to empower you with the knowledge and practical insights needed to design, build, and maintain data pipelines that can not only handle the challenges of today's petabyte era but also pave the way for future data-driven innovation.

CHAPTER ONE

THE RISE OF PETABYTE-SCALE DATA NAVIGATING THE UNCHARTED TERRITORIES OF THE DIGITAL DELUGE

The opening decades of the 21st century have witnessed a transformation of unprecedented scale, a fundamental reshaping of the very fabric of our digital existence. At the heart of this metamorphosis lies an explosive growth in data generation, a phenomenon so profound that it has propelled us into an era defined by petabyte-scale datasets. Organizations across the globe, irrespective of their size or industry, now grapple with daily influxes of information that were once the realm of science fiction. This chapter embarks on a comprehensive exploration of the multifaceted drivers fueling this relentless expansion of the digital universe, meticulously dissecting the key technological and societal forces that have irrevocably altered the landscape of data management. We will delve into the intricate mechanisms by which the burgeoning ecosystem of Internet of Things (IoT) devices, the pervasive influence of social media platforms, the transformative power of artificial intelligence and machine learning (AI/ML), and the imperative for real-time analytics have collectively conspired to unleash this tidal wave of data. Furthermore, we will undertake a critical examination of the inherent limitations and growing inadequacies of traditional data architectures when confronted with datasets of this magnitude, highlighting the fundamental reasons why modern enterprises can no longer afford to cling to outdated paradigms. The chapter will culminate in a compelling argument for a radical rethinking of data pipelines, emphasizing the urgent need for organizations to embrace innovative approaches to data ingestion, processing, storage, and analysis to not only survive the challenges posed by petabyte-scale data but to harness its immense potential to achieve sustained competitive advantage in an increasingly data-centric world.

The Unstoppable Floodgates: Unpacking the Multifarious Drivers of Petabyte Proliferation

The exponential surge in data volumes is not a singular event but rather the confluence of several powerful and interconnected technological advancements and pervasive societal trends. To truly comprehend the magnitude of the petabyte-scale data phenomenon, it is crucial to meticulously dissect the individual contributions of these driving forces.

The relentless proliferation of Internet of Things (IoT) devices stands as a cornerstone of this data explosion. This vast and rapidly expanding network of interconnected physical objects embedded with sensors, software, and other technologies is capable of collecting and exchanging data. From the mundane yet ubiquitous smart home appliances that monitor energy consumption and user preferences to the intricate networks of industrial sensors that optimize manufacturing processes and the increasingly sophisticated wearable technology that tracks our health and activity levels, the sheer diversity and pervasiveness of IoT devices contribute significantly to the data deluge. Connected vehicles, equipped with an array of sensors and communication capabilities, generate massive amounts of data related to navigation, performance, and even driver behavior. The defining characteristic of IoT data is its continuous, granular nature. Each device, often operating autonomously, constantly streams data points, accumulating into colossal datasets over time. As the number of connected devices continues its projected exponential growth, reaching tens of billions in the coming years, the volume of data generated will only intensify, creating an ever-increasing burden on traditional data management systems that were never conceived to handle such relentless and granular streams of information.

Simultaneously, the pervasive and deeply ingrained influence of social media platforms on modern life continues to be a monumental contributor to this exponential data growth. Billions of users across the globe actively engage with these platforms daily, generating an overwhelming variety and volume of predominantly unstructured data. Text posts, status updates, images, videos, live streams, and intricate networks of user interactions, including likes, shares, and comments, all contribute to this massive digital footprint. The velocity at which this social media data is generated is staggering, with millions of posts and interactions occurring every minute. Furthermore, the inherent variety of this data, ranging from simple text to rich multimedia content, presents unique and complex challenges for storage, processing, and meaningful analysis. Extracting valuable insights from this dynamic and often noisy data requires sophisticated techniques that go far beyond the capabilities of traditional relational databases and batch-oriented processing methods. The sheer scale and dynamism of social media data have fundamentally stretched the limits of existing data management capabilities, demanding entirely new approaches to handle its unique characteristics.

The transformative field of artificial intelligence and machine learning (AI/ML) plays a dual role in the rise of petabyte-scale data, acting as both a significant driver of its generation and a voracious consumer of its vast quantities. The development and training of increasingly sophisticated AI/ML models are intrinsically dependent on access to massive datasets. These models, designed to identify intricate patterns, learn complex relationships, and ultimately make intelligent predictions and decisions, require vast amounts of data to achieve accuracy and robustness. The more data an AI/ML algorithm is exposed to, the better it typically performs. As AI/ML becomes increasingly integrated into a widening array of applications across various industries, from personalized recommendations and fraud detection to autonomous systems and medical diagnosis, the insatiable demand for even larger, more diverse, and higher-quality datasets will only continue to escalate. This creates a positive feedback loop, where the need for better AI/ML drives the collection and generation of more data, further contributing to the petabyte-scale data phenomenon.

The ability to gain immediate insights into ongoing operations, real-time customer behavior, and emerging market trends has become a crucial differentiator for maintaining a competitive edge and making timely, data-driven decisions. This imperative for real-time understanding necessitates the ability to ingest, process, and analyze massive volumes of data in near real-time, often as it is being generated. This demand places immense pressure on traditional data infrastructure, which was primarily designed for batch processing and historical analysis. Meeting the requirements of real-time analytics necessitates the adoption of new technologies and architectural patterns capable of handling the high velocity and volume of streaming data, further contributing to the overall growth and complexity of petabyte-scale data management.

The Cracks Beneath the Weight: Exposing the Inherent Limitations of Traditional Data Architectures

Confronted with the relentless and ever-increasing surge of petabyte-scale data, traditional data architectures, which have served organizations for decades, are beginning to exhibit significant and often critical limitations. These established systems, primarily built around relational databases and batch-oriented processing, were simply not designed to handle the sheer volume, velocity, and variety of modern datasets. Understanding these

4

inherent limitations is crucial for recognizing the urgent need for a paradigm shift in data management strategies.

Relational databases, the workhorses of traditional data management, while undeniably robust for structured data and transactional processing, often encounter significant challenges when attempting to scale horizontally to accommodate the immense volume and high velocity of petabyte-scale data. Their architectural design, often based on a scale-up model, makes it difficult and expensive to distribute data and processing across multiple nodes. Furthermore, their rigid schemas, while ensuring data integrity for structured data, become significant bottlenecks when dealing with the diverse and often unstructured nature of data emanating from IoT devices, social media platforms, and AI/ML applications. Querying and analyzing this heterogeneous data using traditional SQL can become complex, inefficient, and time-consuming, hindering the ability to extract timely and meaningful insights.

Furthermore, the traditional Extract, Transform, Load (ETL) processes, which have long been the standard for preparing data for analysis, are fundamentally ill-suited for the demands of real-time analytics and the sheer volume of petabyte-scale data. These batch-oriented processes involve extracting data from source systems, transforming it into a consistent format, and then loading it into a data warehouse at scheduled intervals. The inherent latency associated with these batch cycles means that the data being analyzed is often outdated, rendering it less valuable for time-sensitive decision-making. When dealing with databases, these ETL processes can become incredibly time-consuming and resource-intensive, creating significant delays in accessing and analyzing critical information.

The prevalence of data silos, often an unintended consequence of deploying disparate legacy systems and departmental data management practices, further exacerbates the challenges posed by petabyte-scale data.

These isolated repositories of information prevent a holistic and unified view of organizational data, hindering comprehensive analysis and the identification of valuable cross-functional insights. Integrating data across these silos becomes increasingly complex and resource intensive as data volumes grow, making it difficult to gain a complete and accurate understanding of business performance and customer behavior.

The escalating costs associated with storing and managing petabyte-scale data using traditional on-premises infrastructure present a significant and often unsustainable financial burden for many organizations. The need for continuous and substantial hardware upgrades to accommodate growing data volumes, coupled with the costs of specialized software licenses and the salaries of dedicated IT personnel required to manage these complex systems, can quickly become prohibitive. Moreover, the inherent complexity of managing and maintaining these often-monolithic systems increases the risk of operational inefficiencies, system downtime, and potential data loss, further highlighting the limitations of this traditional approach in the face of petabyte-scale data.

Rethinking the Flow: The Imperative for Modern Data Pipelines in the Petabyte Era

To effectively navigate the complexities and unlock the immense potential of the petabyte-scale data era, modern enterprises must undertake a fundamental and comprehensive rethinking of their approach to data pipelines. The inherent limitations of traditional data architectures, as outlined previously, necessitate a decisive shift towards more scalable, flexible, and agile solutions that are specifically designed to handle the unprecedented volume, velocity, and variety of contemporary data. This transformation requires embracing new architectural paradigms, leveraging cutting-edge technologies, and adopting innovative strategies for data ingestion, processing, storage, and analysis.

Modern data pipelines must be architected with scalability as a foundational principle. They must possess the inherent ability to seamlessly expand their capacity to accommodate ever-increasing data volumes without incurring prohibitive costs or experiencing significant performance degradation. This often involves adopting distributed computing frameworks that can distribute data and processing tasks across a cluster of commodity hardware or leveraging the elastic scalability offered by cloud-based data platforms. Horizontal scaling, the ability to add more nodes to the system as data grows, becomes a critical requirement for managing petabyte-scale data effectively.

Flexibility is another paramount characteristic of modern data pipelines. They must be capable of seamlessly integrating data from a diverse range of sources, including structured databases, unstructured text documents, streaming IoT data, and multimedia content from social media platforms. Furthermore, they must be able to process data in various formats and apply a wide range of transformations and analytical techniques. This requires embracing technologies that can handle schema-on-read approaches and support a variety of data processing paradigms.

Agility is equally crucial in the rapidly evolving landscape of petabyte-scale data. Modern data pipelines must be designed to be adaptable and responsive to changing business needs and technological advancements. Organizations need the ability to quickly and easily modify their data pipelines to incorporate new data sources, implement new analytical models, and adapt to evolving regulatory requirements. This necessitates the adoption of modular architectures, automated deployment processes, and a DevOps culture that fosters collaboration and rapid iteration.

The adoption of innovative technologies and architectural patterns is central to building effective modern data pipelines for petabyte-scale data. Data lakes, which provide a centralized and scalable repository for storing vast amounts of raw data in its native format, offer a more flexible and cost-effective alternative to traditional data warehouses for handling diverse data types. Stream processing engines enable the real-time ingestion and analysis of continuous data streams, empowering organizations with immediate insights and the ability to react to events as they occur. Cloud-based data platforms offer virtually limitless scalability, a wide range of managed data services, and pay-as-you-go pricing models, significantly reducing the operational overhead and upfront investment associated with managing complex data infrastructure. Furthermore, the integration of advanced analytics tools and machine learning platforms directly into the data pipeline enables organizations to derive deeper insights and automate complex decision-making processes at scale.

Staying Competitive in a Data-Intensive World: The Strategic Imperative of Modern Data Management

The dawn of the Petabyte era has irrevocably redefined the competitive landscape, establishing the efficient management and strategic leverage of information as a fundamental differentiator between thriving enterprises and those struggling to remain relevant. In this data-intensive world, the capacity to effectively harness the vast oceans of information flowing through and around organizations is no longer merely an operational advantage; it has become a core strategic imperative. Companies that proactively invest in building scalable and modern data infrastructure are unlocking a wealth of previously unimaginable opportunities, positioning themselves at the forefront of innovation and customer engagement. These forward-thinking organizations are leveraging the power of petabyte-scale data to create hyper-personalized user experiences that resonate deeply with individual customers, implement sophisticated predictive maintenance strategies that minimize downtime and optimize resource allocation, and develop adaptive artificial intelligence models that continuously learn and improve unparalleled insights and automation capabilities.

Conversely, enterprises that continue to cling to outdated and inadequate data management systems face an increasingly precarious future. Unable to effectively process, analyze, and derive meaningful insights from the massive datasets that define the modern business environment, these organizations risk falling further and further behind their more agile and data-savvy competitors. They struggle to keep pace with evolving customer expectations for personalized services and real-time responsiveness, and they miss out on critical opportunities to identify emerging trends, optimize their operations, and develop innovative new products and services. In essence, their inability to navigate the petabyte frontier effectively transforms their data from a potential asset into a significant liability, hindering their agility, stifling their growth, and ultimately threatening their long-term viability.

The transition towards modern data practices is, however, not without its inherent challenges. It necessitates profound cultural shifts within organizations, requiring a fundamental re-evaluation of how data is perceived, valued, and utilized across all departments. It also demands significant financial investment in new technologies, infrastructure, and talent acquisition. Furthermore, it requires the development of new skill sets and expertise within the workforce, as traditional data management roles evolve, and new specializations emerge. Organizations must cultivate a data-driven culture, fostering collaboration between data scientists, engineers, and business stakeholders to effectively translate raw data into actionable intelligence.

Despite these challenges, the potential rewards of embracing modern data practices are immense and far outweigh the costs of inaction. By strategically investing in scalable and flexible data infrastructure, implementing robust data governance frameworks, and cultivating a data-literate workforce, enterprises can transform data from a cumbersome liability into a powerful strategic asset. This transformation fuels innovation by enabling the discovery of previously hidden patterns and insights, enhances agility by providing real-time visibility into key performance indicators, and drives sustainable growth by facilitating data-informed decision-making across all aspects of the business.

This chapter serves as a crucial foundation for the more detailed explorations that will follow. It establishes the critical context of the petabyte era and underscores the strategic importance of modern data management for sustained competitive advantage. As we progress through the subsequent chapters, we will delve into the specific tools, techniques, and architectural patterns that define the modern data stack. We will examine the intricacies of data lakes, data warehouses, stream processing engines, and cloud-based data platforms. Furthermore, we will analyze how leading organizations across various industries are successfully navigating the complexities of the petabyte frontier, providing practical examples and actionable insights into building and leveraging robust modern data infrastructure with confidence and strategic foresight. The journey into the depths of modern data management begins here, with a clear understanding of the high stakes and the immense potential that lies within the effective mastery of petabyte-scale data.

CHAPTER TWO

FUNDAMENTALS OF SCALABLE DATA ARCHITECTURES

The transition to petabyte-scale data has fundamentally challenged the capabilities of traditional data architectures, exposing their inherent limitations in handling the sheer volume, rapid influx, and diverse nature of contemporary data. Organizations that continue to rely on systems conceived for smaller, more stable data environments find themselves increasingly constrained, unable to effectively leverage the vast amounts of information now available. The need for a paradigm shift is undeniable, compelling enterprises to embrace scalable architectures that possess the inherent capacity to expand in tandem with their data growth, adapt seamlessly to fluctuating operational demands, and concurrently support both real-time transactional processes and complex analytical investigations.

Scalability, within this critical context, transcends the simplistic notion of merely augmenting hardware resources. It embodies the fundamental ability of a data architecture to gracefully accommodate escalating data volume, the accelerating velocity of data generation and ingestion, and the increasing variety of data formats and sources without any degradation in crucial performance metrics, system reliability, or overall manageability. It necessitates a holistic approach to system design, one that prioritizes flexibility, modularity, and embedded intelligence, enabling the architecture to dynamically respond to evolving scale requirements. This involves not just the ability to add more processing power or storage capacity, but also the architectural foresight to distribute workloads efficiently, optimize resource utilization, and maintain consistent service levels under varying conditions.

This exploration will delve deeply into the foundational principles that underpin the design and implementation of scalable data architectures. We will examine the essential components that constitute these modern data platforms, understanding their individual roles and how they interoperate to achieve the desired levels of scalability. Furthermore, we will critically analyze the inherent trade-offs associated with different architectural choices, recognizing that the selection of specific technologies and design patterns often involves balancing competing priorities such as cost, complexity, consistency, and latency.

The journey into scalable data architectures will illuminate how contemporary enterprises are strategically structuring their data platforms to achieve resilience, ensuring continuous operation even in the face of failures; embracing distributed computing paradigms to harness the power of networked resources; and increasingly adopting cloud-native approaches that leverage the elasticity and managed services offered by cloud providers. The ultimate goal of these architectural transformations is to establish robust and efficient data pipelines capable of seamlessly ingesting, processing, storing, and serving massive datasets. This capability is not merely a technological imperative but a strategic necessity, empowering organizations to derive timely insights, drive data-driven decision-making, and maintain a competitive edge in an era defined by the exponential growth of data.

Evolution from Monoliths to Distributed Systems

The initial phases of digital transformation witnessed a strong reliance on monolithic database systems and single-node data warehouses as the foundational pillars of data management. These early architectures were characterized by their centralized nature, primarily focused on transactional processing, and meticulously designed to ensure data consistency. Within the context of limited data originating from a relatively small number of internal systems, such as Customer Relationship Management (CRM) platforms, Enterprise Resource Planning (ERP) systems, and basic web server logs, these monolithic systems proved to be adequately functional and manageable.

However, the subsequent explosion in both the sheer volume and the diverse nature of data presented a significant challenge to these established architectures. As organizations began to generate and collect exponentially larger datasets from an expanding array of sources, these once-sufficient monoliths gradually transformed into critical bottlenecks within the data processing pipeline. The primary method of scaling these systems involved vertical scaling, which entailed investing in increasingly powerful and expensive hardware to augment the capabilities of a single server. This approach, however, rapidly encountered inherent physical limitations and prohibitive financial costs, rendering it unsustainable for handling the burgeoning data landscape.

Additionally, the rigid data models enforced by these traditional systems proved to be ill-equipped to accommodate the influx of unstructured and semi-structured data emanating from novel sources. The proliferation of mobile applications, the integration of third-party Application Programming Interfaces (APIs), and the emergence of social media platforms as significant data streams introduced complexities that the fixed schemas of monolithic databases were unable to effectively manage. The need to process and analyze data that did not conform to predefined relational structures highlighted a fundamental inadequacy in the existing architectural paradigm.

This confluence of scalability limitations and data model inflexibility catalyzed a profound shift in architectural thinking, leading to the ascendancy of distributed architectures. In this paradigm, computational workloads and data storage responsibilities are deliberately partitioned and distributed across a multitude of interconnected machines and independent services. Instead of the vertical scaling approach of adding more resources to a single, powerful machine, distributed architectures embrace horizontal scaling, which involves adding more commodity hardware to the distributed network. This fundamental change in scaling strategy unlocks several critical advantages. Distributed systems inherently offer enhanced fault tolerance, as the failure of a single node does not necessarily bring down the entire system. Load balancing mechanisms can be implemented to intelligently distribute incoming requests and processing tasks across the available resources, preventing any single node from becoming overwhelmed. Moreover, distributed architectures facilitate data sharding, a technique that involves partitioning large datasets across multiple storage units, thereby improving query performance and manageability. This distributed approach has now become a foundational principle for any data architecture aspiring to effectively handle and process data at the petabyte scale, providing the necessary resilience and performance to operate under conditions of massive data loads and high concurrency.

Layered Architecture: Breaking Down Complexity

Contemporary scalable data systems are architected based on a layered approach, a fundamental design principle that aims to decompose the inherent complexity of managing vast amounts of data and diverse processing requirements. This architectural strategy involves partitioning the system into distinct layers, each meticulously designed to fulfill a specific set of responsibilities within the overall data lifecycle. These individual layers are not isolated entities but rather interact and communicate with one another through clearly defined and well-established interfaces. This modular design confers several significant advantages, notably enhanced flexibility in adapting to evolving needs, improved isolation of potential failures, ensuring that an issue within one layer is less likely to cascade and impact other parts of the system, and the crucial ability to independently optimize and scale each layer based on its specific performance demands and resource utilization patterns.

The data ingestion layer serves as the initial point of contact and entry for all data entering the system. It is a critical component that must possess the versatility to handle a wide spectrum of data formats, encompassing structured data with well-defined schemas, semi-structured data that may have some organizational properties but lacks a rigid schema, and unstructured data such as text, images, and videos. Furthermore, this layer must seamlessly support both batch processing, where large volumes of data are collected over a period and processed together, and real-time streaming, where data is continuously ingested and processed as it arrives.

Consider, for example, the intricate data ingestion requirements of a modern ride-hailing application. This application needs to simultaneously process a continuous stream of Global Positioning System (GPS) coordinates, transmitted every second from potentially hundreds of thousands of active devices. This real-time data stream is crucial for tracking vehicle locations, calculating estimated times of arrival, and optimizing routing algorithms. Concurrently, the same application might also need to perform nightly batch processing to load historical customer profiles and trip data from a Customer Relationship Management (CRM)

15

system. This batch ingestion process typically involves transferring and transforming large volumes of data according to a predefined schedule.

To address these diverse ingestion needs, a variety of specialized tools and technologies are employed. For managing high-throughput, low-latency real-time event streams, technologies such as Apache Kafka, Confluent (which is built upon Kafka), and Amazon Kinesis provide robust and scalable platforms for data ingestion and distribution. On the other hand, for orchestrating complex batch ingestion workflows and facilitating data routing and transformation, tools like Apache NiFi or Talend offer graphical interfaces and powerful data integration capabilities.

Building a resilient and reliable data ingestion layer necessitates careful consideration of several potential challenges. Data engineers must proactively address issues such as the arrival of data with significant delays (late-arriving data), changes in the structure or format of incoming data over time (schema evolution), the possibility of receiving duplicate messages that could skew analysis, and the need to manage situations where the rate of incoming data exceeds the processing capacity of downstream systems (backpressure). To mitigate these risks and ensure data integrity and system stability, various techniques are employed within the ingestion layer. Stream buffering provides temporary storage for incoming data, allowing downstream systems to catch up during periods of high load. Checkpointing mechanisms track the progress of data processing, enabling recovery from failures without data loss or duplication. Message queues act as intermediaries, decoupling data producers from consumers and providing a mechanism for asynchronous communication and flow control. These strategies are crucial for maintaining the reliability and integrity of the data as they enter the scalable data architecture.

Storage and Lake Architecture

On the concept of storage and lake architecture, the evolution from traditional data warehouses to data lakes and subsequently to the hybrid Lakehouse architecture represents a profound shift in how organizations approach the fundamental challenge of storing and managing their exponentially growing and increasingly diverse data assets. This evolution is not merely a change in technology but reflects a deeper understanding of the varying needs of different data consumers and the imperative to optimize for both cost and analytical agility in the era of big data.

Traditional data warehouses, with their emphasis on schema-on-write, were meticulously designed for Online Analytical Processing (OLAP) workloads. Data was carefully modeled and transformed into relational schemas before being loaded into the warehouse. This rigorous process ensured data consistency and facilitated efficient querying for well-defined business intelligence and reporting needs. Tools and technologies associated with this paradigm, such as relational database management systems (RDBMS) and specialized data warehousing appliances, excelled at providing structured data for generating insights through SQL-based queries. However, the inherent rigidity of this approach presented significant challenges when confronted with the volume and variety of modern data. The time and effort required to model and transform new data sources before ingestion could create bottlenecks, hindering the ability to rapidly explore and analyze novel datasets. Furthermore, the cost of scaling traditional data warehouses, often involving expensive proprietary hardware, became unsustainable as data volumes surged into the petabyte scale.

The emergence of data likes as a viable alternative addressed these limitations head-on. By leveraging the scalability and cost-effectiveness of cloud object storage, data lakes offered a fundamentally different approach to data storage. The principle of schema-on-read aloud organizations to ingest data in its raw, untransformed state, preserving all the nuances and details of the original data source. This flexibility proved invaluable for data scientists and analysts who needed to explore data without the constraints of a predefined schema. The ability to store diverse data formats structured data from relational databases, semi-structured data like JSON and XML from APIs and web applications, and unstructured data such as documents, images, audio, and video within a single, centralized repository opened up new possibilities for advanced analytics, including machine learning and artificial intelligence. The low cost of cloud object storage compared to traditional data warehousing solutions also made data lakes an economically attractive option for storing vast quantities of data.

However, the very flexibility that made data lakes appealing also introduced new challenges. The lack of enforced schemas and transactional consistency could lead to data swamps, where data lacked governance, quality, and discoverability. Without robust data management capabilities, it became difficult to ensure the reliability and trustworthiness of the data stored in the lake, particularly for critical business applications that required data integrity. Querying data in a schema-on-read environment could also be less performant for certain analytical workloads that benefited from the structured organization of a data warehouse.

The Lakehouse architecture represents an innovative convergence of the strengths of both data lakes and data warehouses, aiming to overcome their respective limitations. Platforms like Databricks Delta Lake, built on top of Apache Spark and cloud object storage, and Apache Iceberg, an open table format for data lakes, introduce a transactional layer to the data lake. This transactional layer brings ACID properties to data lake storage, ensuring data consistency and reliability even with concurrent read and write operations. This is a significant departure from the eventual consistency models often associated with basic object storage.

Furthermore, Lakehouse architectures enable schema evolution and enforcement directly on the data lake. While still retaining the flexibility to store raw data, they allow for the definition and enforcement of schemas for specific datasets or tables within the lake, improving data quality and facilitating more efficient querying for downstream analytical processes. Data versioning capabilities, another key feature of lakehouse platforms, provide a complete history of changes to the data, enabling auditing, reproducibility of analyses, and the ability to roll back to previous versions if necessary.

The adoption of lakehouse architectures signifies a recognition that a one-size-fits-all approach to data storage is no longer viable in the face of petabyte-scale data and diverse analytical requirements. By combining the scalability and flexibility of data lakes with the performance and governance features of data warehouses, lakehouse platforms provide a unified foundation for a wide range of data workloads, from exploratory data science and real-time analytics to traditional business intelligence and machine learning. This unified approach simplifies data management, reduces data silos, and empowers organizations to derive greater value from their vast data assets in a cost-effective and scalable manner.

Processing and Compute Layer

The processing and computing layer within a modern scalable data architecture is the engine room where raw, ingested data is transformed into actionable insights. This layer is responsible for applying a wide array of operations, including filtering irrelevant information, transforming data into usable formats, aggregating granular details into meaningful summaries, and joining disparate datasets to create richer contextual understanding. The processing within this layer can be broadly categorized into two primary paradigms, each catering to distinct latency and analytical requirements: batch processing, which operates on large volumes of data at scheduled intervals, and stream processing, which handles continuous data flows in near real time.

Batch processing is the workhorse for handling massive historical datasets. It typically involves executing long-running jobs that process terabytes or even petabytes of data. To achieve the necessary scalability and performance for such large-scale computations, batch processing frameworks like Apache Spark, Apache Hive (often used with Spark or MapReduce), and Google Dataflow employ a distributed computing model. These systems intelligently divide a large processing job into numerous smaller, independent tasks and distribute these tasks across a cluster of worker nodes. This parallelization of computation allows for the efficient utilization of resources and significantly reduces the overall processing time for complex data transformations. For instance, a large e-commerce company might use batch processing overnight to analyze the previous day's sales transactions, calculate key performance indicators (KPIs), generate reports on product performance, and prepare data for downstream analytical dashboards. The ability to scale out by adding more nodes to the processing cluster makes these systems highly adaptable to increasing data volumes.

In contrast to the periodic nature of batch processing, stream processing systems are designed to handle continuous streams of data with minimal latency. Frameworks such as Apache Flink, Kafka Streams (tightly integrated with Apache Kafka), and Apache Beam (which can support both batch and streaming) enable the development of event-driven architectures. These systems continuously consume data as it arrives from various sources, often through message brokers like Kafka, apply predefined transformations and business logic, and publish the resulting processed data to downstream systems or applications. Stream processing is crucial for use cases that demand immediate insights and actions based on real-time events. Examples include detecting fraudulent transactions as they occur, identifying anomalies in system behavior in real time, updating product recommendations on an e-commerce website based on immediate user interactions, and analyzing telemetry data from Internet of Things (IoT) devices to trigger immediate responses or alerts. The ability to process events with very low latency is a defining characteristic of stream processing.

Given the critical nature of data processing, scalable processing systems must incorporate robust mechanisms to ensure fault tolerance. Failures of individual nodes in a distributed processing cluster are inevitable, and the system must be designed to handle these failures gracefully without interrupting the overall processing or losing data. Techniques like checkpointing, where the state of a running computation is periodically saved, and event replay, which allows for the reprocessing of data from a known good state in case of a failure, are essential for achieving fault tolerance.

Furthermore, these systems must often provide strong guarantees regarding the processing of data, such as exactly once processing. This guarantee ensures that each data record is processed exactly one time, neither duplicated nor lost, even in the face of system failures or retries. Achieving exactly once semantics in a distributed streaming environment is a complex technical challenge that requires careful coordination between data sources, processing engines, and data sinks. Frameworks like Flink and Kafka Streams implement sophisticated mechanisms, such as transactional writes and idempotent operations, to provide these strong consistency guarantees, which are crucial for applications where data accuracy and integrity are paramount, such as financial transactions or critical sensor readings. The choice between batch and stream processing, or often a combination of both (a lambda or kappa architecture), depends heavily on the specific requirements of the data processing task, particularly the desired latency and the nature of the data being analyzed.

Modern data architectures often leverage both paradigms to provide a comprehensive view of data, combining historical insights from batch processing with real-time awareness from stream processing.

Serving and Access Layer

The Serving and Access Layer represents the culmination of the data pipeline, acting as the gateway through which processed and curated data is made available to a diverse range of consumers, including end-users performing business intelligence analysis, various internal and external applications requiring data integration, and sophisticated machine learning algorithms that leverage the processed information for model training and inference. This layer is characterized by critical performance requirements, including the ability to handle high concurrency to support numerous simultaneous requests, the necessity for low latency to provide responsive data access, and the implementation of fine-grained access control mechanisms to ensure data security and compliance.

Modern data warehouses, such as Snowflake, Google BigQuery, and Amazon Redshift, are specifically engineered to serve analytical workloads on a scale. These platforms have evolved significantly from traditional data warehouses, incorporating architectural innovations that optimize query performance on massive datasets. Columnar storage, a key feature, organizes data by columns rather than rows, which significantly improves the efficiency of analytical queries that typically involve aggregations and filtering on a subset of columns. Vectorized execution further enhances performance by processing data in batches or vectors, reducing the overhead of individual row-based operations. Intelligent caching mechanisms store frequently accessed data in memory or on faster storage tiers, minimizing the need to retrieve data from disk for subsequent queries. Sophisticated query optimizers analyze SQL queries and generate efficient execution plans, often leveraging techniques like predicate pushdown and join reordering to minimize data scanning and processing. Furthermore, these cloud-native data warehouses offer auto-scaling capabilities, allowing computing resources to be dynamically adjusted up or down based on the intensity of the analytical workload, ensuring optimal performance and cost efficiency.

Beyond direct analytical access through data warehouses, the Serving and Access Layer also encompasses mechanisms for exposing data to applications and external consumers. APIs (Application Programming Interfaces) and microservices have become prevalent patterns for providing programmatic access to data. RESTful APIs, with their stateless nature and reliance on standard HTTP methods, are widely used for building interoperable services. GraphQL, an alternative API query language, offers clients the flexibility to request only the specific data they need, reducing over-fetching and improving performance, particularly in complex data relationships. To further enhance response times and reduce the load on backend data stores, caching layers, often implemented using in-memory data stores like Redis or Memcached, are frequently deployed in front of APIs. These coaches store frequently requested data, allowing subsequent requests to be served directly from the cache with significantly lower latency.

A paramount concern within the Serving and Access Layer is ensuring secure and compliant data access. Robust security measures are essential to protect sensitive information and adhere to regulatory requirements. Identity management systems are used to authenticate users and applications attempting to access data. Role-Based Access Control (RBAC) mechanisms define permissions based on the roles assigned to users or applications, allowing for fine-grained control over what data and operations are accessible. Data masking techniques can be employed to redact or obfuscate sensitive data fields for users who do not have the necessary privileges, while still allowing them to work with the data for analytical or application purposes. Comprehensive audit logging tracks data access and modifications, providing a detailed history for security monitoring, compliance reporting, and forensic analysis. These security controls must be consistently enforced across all access points within the Serving and Access Layer.

Metadata, Governance, and Observability in Detail:

As data ecosystems expand in scale and complexity, the ability to effectively manage and understand the data becomes increasingly challenging. This necessitates a robust Metadata layer, which goes beyond simply tracking technical details like schemas, data formats, and storage locations. Comprehensive metadata management also includes capturing business context, such as data definitions, data ownership, data lineage (tracing the origin and transformations of data), and data quality rules.

Dedicated metadata platforms, such as Amundsen (developed by Lyft), DataHub (developed by LinkedIn), and commercial solutions like Collibra, provide organizations with a unified catalog of their data assets. These platforms enable data discovery, allowing users to easily find and understand the data they need. They also facilitate the enforcement of data quality rules, ensuring that data meets defined standards before being consumed. Crucially, metadata platforms track data lineage, providing a clear audit trail of how data has been transformed and moved through the system. This lineage information is invaluable for debugging data quality issues, understanding the impact of data changes, and ensuring compliance with data governance regulations.

Complementing metadata management, Observability forms another critical layer for maintaining control and ensuring the health and performance of scalable data architectures. These complex systems generate vast amounts of operational data, including logs (detailed records of events), metrics (numerical measurements of system performance), and traces (detailed execution paths of requests across different services). This observability data must be effectively collected, stored, and analyzed to provide insights into the system's behavior.

Tools like Prometheus (for collecting and storing metrics), Grafana (for visualizing metrics and logs), and Open Telemetry (an open-source standard for telemetry data) are widely adopted for building observability solutions. Proactive monitoring of key metrics, such as CPU utilization, memory consumption, network latency, and query performance, allows operations teams to identify potential issues before they impact users. Capacity planning relies on analyzing historical trends in resource utilization to forecast future needs and ensure the system can handle growing data volumes and processing demands. Anomaly detection algorithms can be applied to observability data to automatically identify unusual patterns that might indicate performance bottlenecks, security breaches, or system failures. Effective observability is essential for maintaining the stability, performance, and reliability of petabyte-scale data architectures.

Design Patterns for Scalability

The Serving and Access Layer represents the critical juncture where the vast amounts of data, meticulously ingested, processed, and stored in the preceding layers, are finally made available for consumption and utilization. It is the outward-facing component of the scalable data architecture, designed to cater to the diverse needs of end-users performing analytical explorations, internal and external applications requiring seamless data integration, and sophisticated algorithms driving advanced analytics and machine learning initiatives. The fundamental requirements for this layer revolve around its ability to handle a high volume of concurrent requests without performance degradation, provide data access with minimal latency to ensure responsiveness, and enforce granular access controls to safeguard data security and maintain compliance with relevant regulations.

Modern data warehouses have evolved to become highly sophisticated platforms optimized for serving analytical workloads at scale. Offerings like Snowflake, Google BigQuery, and Amazon Redshift are prime examples of this evolution. Their architectural underpinnings are specifically tailored to execute complex analytical queries efficiently over massive datasets. Columnar storage is a cornerstone of their design, organizing data by columns rather than traditional rows. This optimization significantly enhances the performance of analytical queries that typically involve aggregating or filtering specific columns, as it reduces the amount of data that needs to be read from storage. Vectorized execution further accelerates query processing by operating on batches of data values simultaneously, minimizing processing overhead. Intelligent caching mechanisms are employed to store frequently accessed data in faster memory tiers, reducing the need for repeated disk I/O and dramatically improving query response times. Furthermore, sophisticated query optimizers analyze incoming SQL queries, generating efficient execution plans that leverage techniques like data partitioning, indexing, and join optimization to minimize resource consumption and maximize speed. A crucial aspect of these modern data warehouses is their support for auto-scaling compute resources. This elasticity allows the platform to dynamically adjust the amount of processing power allocated based on the current workload intensity, ensuring consistent performance during peak demand periods while optimizing costs during quieter times.

Beyond direct analytical querying through data warehouses, the Serving and Access Layer also encompasses the mechanisms for exposing data programmatically to a wider range of applications and external consumers. APIs and microservices have become the dominant paradigms for facilitating this data integration. RESTful APIs, adhering to stateless communication principles and leveraging standard HTTP methods, provide a widely adopted and interoperable means for accessing and manipulating data. GraphQL offers a more flexible alternative, empowering clients to specify precisely the data they require in a single query, thereby reducing over-fetching and improving application performance, especially in scenarios involving complex data relationships and nested structures. To further enhance the responsiveness of these APIs and microservices, caching layers are frequently implemented. In-memory data stores like Redis or Memcached are commonly used for this purpose, storing frequently requested data closer to the application layer and serving subsequent requests directly from the cache with significantly lower latency than retrieving it from the underlying data store.

Ensuring secure and compliant access to the server data is of paramount importance within this layer. A multi-faceted approach to security is essential. Robust identity management systems are implemented to authenticate users and applications attempting to access data, verifying their credentials before granting access. Role-Based Access Control (RBAC) frameworks are then employed to define granular permissions based on the roles assigned to users or applications, dictating precisely which data resources and operations they are authorized to access. Data masking techniques provide an additional layer of security by selectively redacting or obfuscating sensitive data fields for users who do not possess the necessary privileges, allowing them to work with the data for legitimate purposes without exposing confidential information. Finally, comprehensive audit logging mechanisms are implemented to meticulously track all data access attempts and modifications, providing a detailed historical record that is crucial for security monitoring, compliance reporting to regulatory bodies, and forensic analysis in the event of security incidents. These security measures must be consistently applied and enforced across all entry points within the Serving and Access Layer to maintain the integrity and confidentiality of the data.

Metadata, Governance, and Observability in Detail:

As data ecosystems scale to encompass the petabytes of information and involve numerous interconnected systems, the challenge of maintaining control and understanding becomes exponentially more complex. This is where the critical importance of Metadata, Governance, and Observability layers comes into sharp focus.

Metadata management transcends the mere cataloging of technical specifications such as data schemas, file formats, and storage locations. A comprehensive metadata strategy also encompasses capturing vital business context. This includes defining clear business glossaries and data dictionaries to ensure a common understanding of data elements across the organization, establishing clear data ownership to assign responsibility and accountability, and meticulously tracking data lineage to understand the origin and transformations applied to any given dataset.

Dedicated metadata platforms, such as the open-source Amundsen and DataHub, alongside commercial solutions like Collibra, provide organizations with centralized and unified catalogs of their diverse data assets. These platforms empower users to easily discover the data they need through intuitive search and browsing capabilities. They also facilitate the enforcement of data quality rules, allowing data stewards to define and monitor data quality metrics and ensure that data meets established standards before being used for critical decision-making. The ability to trace the origin and flow of any dataset through data lineage is particularly crucial for auditing purposes, allowing organizations to demonstrate compliance with regulatory requirements and understand the impact of data changes. Furthermore, data lineage is invaluable for debugging data quality issues, enabling data engineers to pinpoint the source of errors in the data pipeline.

Observability forms another indispensable layer for ensuring the health, performance, and reliability of complex, scalable data architectures. These systems generate a continuous stream of operational data, including detailed logs of system activities, granular metrics capturing performance indicators like CPU utilization, memory consumption, network latency, and query execution times, and distributed traces that provide end-to-end visibility into the execution paths of requests across multiple services. This wealth of observability data must be effectively collected, aggregated, stored, and analyzed to provide actionable insights into the system's behavior.

Tools like Prometheus, an open-source monitoring and alerting system, are widely used for collecting and storing time-series metrics. Grafana provides powerful visualization capabilities, allowing teams to create interactive dashboards to monitor key performance indicators and identify trends or anomalies. Open Telemetry offers a standardized framework for generating and collecting telemetry data (logs, metrics, and traces) in a vendor-agnostic manner. Proactive monitoring of these observability signals enables operations teams to identify potential issues, such as performance bottlenecks or system errors, before they escalate and impact end-users. Analyzing historical trends in resource utilization is essential for effective capacity planning, ensuring that the infrastructure can adequately support future data growth and processing demands. Moreover, applying anomaly detection algorithms to observability data can automatically identify unusual patterns or deviations from normal behavior, potentially indicating underlying problems or even security threats. A robust observability strategy is therefore fundamental for maintaining the stability, optimizing the performance, and ensuring the overall reliability of petabyte-scale data architectures.

Challenges and Trade-Offs

Designing and implementing data architectures that can seamlessly scale to handle petabyte-scale data introduces a new set of intricate challenges and necessitates careful consideration of inherent trade-offs. The distributed nature of these modern systems, while providing the necessary scalability and resilience, often introduces complexities that were less prevalent in traditional monolithic architectures.

One common challenge in distributed systems is the inherent tendency for data duplication. As data is replicated across multiple nodes for fault tolerance and to improve read performance, the risk of inconsistencies and storage inefficiencies increases. This necessitates the implementation of robust deduplication strategies to identify and eliminate redundant data, ensuring data integrity and optimizing storage utilization. These strategies can range from periodic batch processes that scan for and merge duplicate records to more sophisticated real-time mechanisms that prevent duplicates from being written in the first place. Choosing the appropriate deduplication strategy involves balancing the computational cost of deduplication against the potential risks and costs associated with data redundancy.

Another fundamental trade-off in designing scalable data systems is the tension between latency and consistency. In systems that prioritize real-time data processing and low-latency access, achieving strong consistency (where all reads reflect the most recent writes) across a distributed environment can introduce significant performance overhead. To maintain responsiveness, such systems might opt for eventual consistency, where data changes may take some time to propagate across all nodes. While this approach enhances performance and availability, it introduces the possibility of temporary inconsistencies, where different users or applications might see slightly different versions of the data. The choice between strong and eventual consistency depends heavily on the specific use case and the tolerance for temporary data discrepancies. Applications requiring strict data accuracy, such as financial transactions, typically necessitate strong consistency, even if it comes at the cost of higher latency. Conversely, applications like social media feeds might tolerate eventual consistency in favor of faster updates and higher availability.

Cost control presents another significant challenge in the realm of scalable data architectures, particularly in cloud-based environments. While the elasticity offered by cloud providers allows for on-demand scaling of resources, this flexibility can also lead to uncontrolled resource consumption and spiraling costs if not managed effectively. Careful monitoring of resource utilization, implementation of cost allocation strategies, and the establishment of automated scaling policies with defined upper bounds are crucial for preventing cost sprawl. Organizations need to adopt a cost-aware culture and continuously optimize their data pipelines and storage configurations to ensure cost efficiency.

Beyond the technical challenges, building and operating scalable data systems requires a significant investment in the right skills and fostering a collaborative culture within the organization. These complex architectures necessitate cross-functional expertise, bringing together data engineers responsible for building and maintaining the data pipelines, Site Reliability Engineers (SREs) focused on system stability and performance, DevOps engineers who automate infrastructure and deployment processes, and security teams who ensure data protection and compliance. Effective collaboration and communication between these teams are essential for the successful development and operation of scalable data platforms. Furthermore, organizations must embrace modern software development practices for their data pipelines, including the use of version control systems to track changes, the implementation of Continuous Integration/Continuous Delivery (CI/CD) pipelines for automated testing and deployment, and the creation of comprehensive documentation to ensure maintainability and knowledge sharing.

Looking towards the future, the evolution of scalable data platforms is likely to be shaped by the increasing prevalence of autonomous systems. The vision is of data platforms that can self-optimize their performance, automatically scale resources in response to changing demands, and proactively detect and mitigate potential failures before they impact operations. Advancements in Artificial Intelligence (AI) and Machine Learning (ML) will play a crucial role in realizing this vision, enabling architectures to become more intelligent. These intelligent platforms will be capable of predicting future demand patterns, recommending optimal indexing strategies for improved query performance, and dynamically rerouting traffic to maintain high availability.

Another significant trend in the future of scalable data platforms is the growing convergence between analytical and operational workloads. Traditionally, analytical processing (OLAP) and transactional processing (OLTP) were handled by separate, specialized systems. However, technologies like Hybrid Transactional and Analytical Processing (HTAP) are emerging, which aim to enable real-time insights directly from operational data. By blurring the lines between transactional and analytical systems, HTAP promises to provide organizations with timelier and context-aware insights without the need for complex and often delayed data movement between separate systems.

Finally, the rise of edge computing and decentralized data models will necessitate data architectures that can support hybrid scalability. Organizations will increasingly need to handle both centralized, cloud-scale operations for large-scale data processing and storage, as well as distributed micro-processing at the edge, closer to the data sources. This hybrid approach will require new architectural patterns and technologies that can seamlessly integrate and manage data across diverse environments, from centralized cloud infrastructure to geographically distributed edge devices.

CHAPTER THREE

DESIGNING FOR FAULT TOLERANCE AND RESILIENCE

The transition to managing data at the petabyte scale marks a significant inflection point in the realm of data architecture. It moves us beyond the traditional concerns of efficient processing and storage into a domain where the sheer magnitude and distributed nature of systems introduce an entirely new dimension of complexity: the inevitability of failure. In this extended exploration of fault tolerance and resilience, we delve deeper into the underlying philosophies, intricate design patterns, and critical considerations that must guide the construction of data platforms capable of sustaining operations amidst the constant churn of hardware degradation, network anomalies, and software imperfections. The ability to not only withstand these disruptions but also to gracefully recover and maintain data integrity and service availability is no longer a desirable attribute; it is a fundamental prerequisite for any organization operating at this data echelon.

The Shifting Paradigm: From Failure Prevention to Failure Management

The foundational principles that guided historical system design often revolved around the aspirational, yet ultimately unattainable, goal of complete failure prevention. This paradigm emphasized the meticulous selection of high-grade hardware components, the implementation of exhaustive testing protocols across the entire software development lifecycle, and the adherence to rigorous software engineering best practices. The underlying assumption was that by diligently adhering to these principles, systems could be made sufficiently robust to avoid significant operational disruptions. While these preventative measures remain absolutely critical as the first line of defense in building reliable systems, the sheer magnitude and intricate interconnectedness characteristic of petabyte-level deployments render this singular focus on prevention fundamentally inadequate.

The stark reality at this scale is dictated by the unyielding statistical laws of large numbers. When dealing with infrastructures comprising thousands, and often tens of thousands, of individual but interdependent components ranging from physical servers and vast storage arrays to complex network switches and intricate software modules the probability of one or more of these elements encountering a fault within any reasonable operational timeframe escalates dramatically. The failure of a single disk drive, once a relatively isolated incident, becomes a predictable and recurring event within a massive storage cluster. Transient disruptions in network links, which might have been infrequent blips in smaller networks, become a constant background noise in sprawling, distributed environments. Even the most rigorously tested and seemingly bug-free software will inevitably reveal latent defects under the unique and often unpredictable load conditions inherent in petabyte-scale data processing and access patterns. These issues, which might have remained dormant or manifested as minor anomalies in smaller systems, can have cascading and potentially catastrophic consequences in the interconnected web of a large-scale deployment.

Therefore, the traditional design philosophy, which is primarily aimed at preventing failures, must undergo a profound and fundamental shift. The central focus must transition from this aspirational, albeit ultimately limited, goal of complete failure prevention to the pragmatic and proactive reality of comprehensive failure management. This necessitates architecting systems with the explicit and unwavering understanding that failures are not isolated exceptions to the norm but rather anticipated and statistically probable occurrences within the operational lifecycle. The primary objective then evolves beyond simply avoiding breakdowns to minimizing the detrimental impact of these inevitable failures on the core tenets of data availability (ensuring data remains accessible when needed), data integrity (preserving the accuracy and consistency of the data), and overall system functionality (maintaining the ability to perform its intended tasks).

Resilience, in this evolved context, transcends the more limited concept of mere fault tolerance. While fault tolerance focuses on the system's ability to continue operating in the immediate presence of a fault, resilience encompasses a broader set of capabilities. It includes not only the ability to withstand failures without immediate catastrophic consequences but also the inherent capacity to self-heal by automatically recovering from faults, adapt to changing operational conditions and resource availability, and ultimately return to a stable and healthy operational state with minimal or, ideally, no manual intervention. Achieving this level of resilience necessitates a deep and nuanced understanding of the various potential failure modes that can manifest at petabyte scale, the meticulous implementation of robust and multi-layered mitigation strategies designed to address these specific failure types, and the cultivation of a proactive operational mindset that anticipates and prepares for the inevitable disruptions. This proactive stance involves continuous monitoring, automated alerting, and well-rehearsed recovery procedures, moving away from a reactive "fix it when it breaks" mentality towards an anticipatory "prepare for it before it happens" approach

Expanding on Core Principles: A Holistic Approach to Resilience

The core principles of fault-tolerant design, as previously introduced, form the bedrock upon which resilient petabyte-scale systems are built. However, at this scale, these principles demand a more nuanced and comprehensive interpretation:

While basic duplication of data and components is a starting point, advanced redundancy strategies involve intelligent distribution and management of replicas. Considerations include the optimal number of replicas (balancing fault tolerance with storage overhead and write latency), the geographical distribution of replicas to protect against regional outages, and the mechanisms for ensuring consistency across replicas. Techniques like erasure coding, which provides data redundancy with lower storage overhead than full replication, become increasingly important at petabyte scale. Furthermore, the system must have automated mechanisms for detecting failed replicas and seamlessly initiating the creation of new ones to maintain the desired level of redundancy.

Effective isolation goes beyond modular design. It involves the careful partitioning of resources (CPU, memory, network bandwidth) between different components and services to prevent resource exhaustion in one area from impacting others. Containerization and virtualization technologies play a crucial role in enforcing these boundaries. Moreover, circuit breaker patterns, as discussed later, are a form of temporal isolation, preventing repeated failed attempts from overwhelming a failing service and potentially causing cascading failures in dependent systems.

Self-healing capabilities in petabyte-scale systems must be highly automated and proactive. This includes automatic detection of failed nodes or services, seamless failover to standby replicas or alternative resources, automated restart of failed processes, and sophisticated data repair mechanisms that can identify and correct data corruption using redundant copies or parity information. The speed and efficiency of these self-healing processes are critical for minimizing downtime and maintaining data integrity at scale.

At petabyte scale, simply monitoring basic system metrics is insufficient. A comprehensive observability strategy is required, encompassing detailed logging, granular metrics collection, distributed tracing to understand request flow across services, and sophisticated anomaly detection algorithms. These tools enable proactive identification of subtle performance degradations or unusual patterns that might precede a full-blown failure. Intelligent alerting systems must be configured to notify the right teams with actionable information, allowing for timely intervention and preventing minor issues from escalating into major outages. Predictive analytics, leveraging historical observability data, can even be employed to anticipate potential failures before they occur, enabling proactive maintenance and capacity adjustments.

Deep Dive into Fault-Tolerant Design Patterns: Practical Implementations

The core principles translate into a set of powerful design patterns that are widely adopted in building resilient petabyte-scale systems: The choice of replication strategy is a nuanced decision with significant implications for system behavior. Synchronous replication, while ensuring strong consistency, can introduce unacceptable latency, especially in geographically distributed systems. Asynchronous replication offers lower latency and higher availability but necessitates mechanisms for handling potential data inconsistencies, such as read-after-write consistency models or eventual consistency with reconciliation processes. Quorum-based replication, where a majority of replicas must agree on a write operation, provides a tunable balance between consistency and availability, as defined by the read and write quorums. For instance, a write quorum of $(n/2 + 1)$ and a read quorum of $(n/2 + 1)$ in a system with 'n' replicas ensures consistency, as any read operation will overlap with at least one successful write.

In distributed processing frameworks like Apache Spark or Flink, checkpointing involves not just saving the state of individual tasks but also coordinating the checkpointing process across the entire distributed computation. This often involves distributed consensus protocols to ensure that the global state is consistent at the checkpoint. The storage of checkpoints must also be highly reliable and scalable, often utilizing distributed file systems or object storage. Incremental checkpointing, where only the changes to the state since the last checkpoint are saved, can help reduce the overhead of frequent checkpointing in large-scale computations.

Achieving idempotency in complex distributed systems often requires careful design of APIs and data processing logic. For example, instead of simply incrementing a counter, an idempotent operation might set the counter to a specific value if it's below a certain threshold. Utilizing unique identifiers for requests and tracking the processing status of requests can also help ensure idempotency. Message queues with at-least-once delivery semantics often rely on idempotent consumers to handle potential duplicate messages without causing unintended side effects.

Implementing a circuit breaker effectively requires careful tuning of its parameters, such as the failure threshold, the retry interval, and the fallback mechanism. Fallback mechanisms can range from returning cached data to providing a degraded but functional service. Monitoring the state of the circuit breaker (closed, open, half-open) is also crucial for understanding the health of dependent services.

Implementing bulkheads can involve using separate thread pools for different services, isolating network connections, or even deploying services in separate containers or virtual machines with dedicated resource limits. This prevents a resource exhaustion issue in one service from starving other critical services. Careful capacity planning is essential to ensure that each bulkhead has sufficient resources to handle its expected workload.

Lessons from the Trenches: Extended Case Studies

To truly grasp the practical application and profound impact of fault-tolerant design principles at petabyte scale, a deeper examination of the strategies employed by industry leaders like Google and Netflix is invaluable. These organizations, operating at the very forefront of data management and service delivery, have not only encountered the challenges of massive scale but have also pioneered innovative approaches to engineer remarkable levels of resilience into their complex systems. Their experiences offer concrete examples and crucial insights for anyone embarking on the journey of building and maintaining robust data platforms.

Google's approach to reliability is deeply ingrained in its engineering culture and permeates every layer of its infrastructure. Their orchestration systems, Borg (the precursor to Kubernetes) and Kubernetes itself, are prime examples of designing for inherent fault tolerance in resource management and workload scheduling. These systems continuously monitor the health of containers and the underlying nodes they run on. Upon detecting a failure – be it a crashed application, an unresponsive container, or a failing hardware node – they automatically initiate rescheduling of the affected workloads onto healthy and available resources. This self-healing capability minimizes downtime and ensures that critical services remain operational even in the face of individual component failures. The abstraction layer provided by these orchestrators shields applications from the complexities of the underlying infrastructure, allowing developers to focus on their core logic while relying on the platform to handle resource management and basic fault recovery.

Their distributed storage systems, such as the globally distributed Spanner database, exemplify sophisticated replication and consistency mechanisms designed for extreme data durability and high availability across geographically dispersed data centers. Spanner employs synchronous replication across a majority of replicas within a Paxos group to ensure strong consistency, even in the presence of network partitions. This guarantees that data writes are durable and that reads reflect the latest committed state, regardless of which replica is accessed within the quorum. Furthermore, Spanner utilizes atomic commits across multiple Paxos groups to provide globally consistent transactions, a remarkable feat at planetary scale that underscores their commitment to data integrity. The automated mechanisms for detecting and replacing failed storage nodes, coupled with continuous data integrity checks and repair processes, further contribute to the resilience of their storage infrastructure.

The Site Reliability Engineering (SRE) teams at Google play a pivotal role in maintaining and improving system reliability. Their culture emphasizes a data-driven approach to operations, with Service Level Objectives (SLOs) and Service Level Indicators (SLIs) serving as key metrics for defining and measuring system performance and reliability. A crucial aspect of their practice is the blameless postmortem analysis conducted after any incident. The focus is not on assigning blame but on understanding the root causes of failures, identifying areas for improvement in system design and operational processes, and implementing preventative measures to mitigate the risk of similar incidents in the future. This culture of continuous learning and improvement is a cornerstone of Google's ability to maintain high levels of reliability across their vast and complex infrastructure. Moreover, their commitment to automation extends beyond workload orchestration to encompass a wide range of recovery procedures, such as automated failover, rollback of faulty deployments, and automated scaling of resources in response to increased load or detected anomalies. This minimizes the need for manual intervention during critical situations, reducing the potential for human error and accelerating the time to recover.

Netflix has taken a uniquely proactive and arguably more radical approach to engineering resilience, famously embodied by their Simian Army. This suite of tools goes beyond simply simulating common failure scenarios; it actively injects various types of failures into their live production environment. Chaos Monkey, the original and perhaps most well-known member of the Simian Army, randomly terminates virtual machine instances in their Amazon Web Services (AWS) infrastructure. This forces their engineering teams to build systems that are inherently tolerant of instance failures, with automated mechanisms for detecting the loss of an instance and seamlessly replacing it without impacting the user experience.

Over time, the Simian Army has evolved to include a diverse range of "monkeys" designed to simulate more nuanced and challenging failure modes. Latency Monkey introduces artificial delays in network communication to test the system's ability to handle slow or unreliable connections. Chaos Gorilla simulates the failure of an entire availability zone within AWS, forcing them to ensure that their architecture can gracefully failover across different zones. Doctor Monkey proactively monitors the health of instances and services, identifying potential issues before they escalate into full-blown failures and attempting automated remediation. Conformity Monkey ensures that instances adhere to best practices and compliance standards. This proactive and continuous approach to failure testing has deeply ingrained a culture of resilience engineering throughout the organization, making it a core consideration in every stage of its development lifecycle.

Beyond proactive failure testing, Netflix also heavily relies on architectural patterns that promote resilience. Their transition from a monolithic application to a microservices-based architecture was driven in part by the need for greater fault isolation. By breaking down their application into a collection of independent services, a failure in one service is less likely to cascade and bring down the entire platform. They also heavily leverage reactive programming models and asynchronous communication (often using message queues) to build loosely coupled services that can operate independently and are more resilient to the temporary unavailability of other services.

Their extensive use of edge caching and content delivery networks (CDNs) plays a crucial role in insulating their core infrastructure from massive spikes in user traffic and potential network disruptions between users and their servers. By distributing content geographically closer to users, they reduce latency and improve the overall streaming experience, while also offloading a significant amount of traffic from their origin servers. Furthermore, Netflix has invested heavily in building detailed monitoring dashboards and sophisticated alerting systems that provide real-time visibility into the health and performance of their vast distributed system. These tools enable their operations teams to rapidly detect anomalies, diagnose the root causes of issues, and implement effective mitigation strategies, often before users even notice a problem.

The experiences of Google and Netflix underscore the critical importance of a proactive and multifaceted approach to engineering resilience at petabyte scale. Google emphasizes building reliability into the very fabric of their infrastructure through robust orchestration, sophisticated data replication, a strong SRE culture, and extensive automation of recovery processes.

Netflix takes a more aggressive approach by actively injecting failures into their production environment to force the development of inherently fault-tolerant systems, coupled with architectural patterns that promote isolation and the strategic use of caching and CDNs. While their specific strategies may differ, both organizations demonstrate that building resilient petabyte-scale data platforms requires a deep understanding of potential failure modes, a commitment to continuous testing and improvement, and a cultural mindset that embraces failure as an inevitable aspect of operating at such an immense scale. Their lessons from the trenches provide invaluable guidance for anyone striving to build data systems that can not only handle massive data loads but also gracefully weather the inevitable storms of distributed computing.

The Ongoing Evolution: Towards Self-Healing and Adaptive Systems

The relentless pursuit of greater reliability and efficiency in petabyte-scale data systems is driving a continuous cycle of innovation in fault tolerance and resilience. The future landscape of these architectures is increasingly characterized by the integration of sophisticated intelligence, moving beyond purely reactive measures towards proactive prediction and autonomous remediation. The next generation of resilient data platforms will leverage the power of machine learning (ML) and artificial intelligence (AI) to anticipate potential failures, dynamically adapt to changing conditions, and even autonomously heal themselves, ushering in an era of truly intelligent resilience.

One of the most promising trends is the increasing use of ML and AI to analyze the vast streams of telemetry data generated by these complex systems. By ingesting and processing historical logs, performance metrics, and even anomaly patterns, ML models can be trained to identify subtle indicators that might precede a hardware failure, a network congestion issue, or a software anomaly. This predictive capability allows for proactive maintenance interventions, such as preemptively migrating workloads away from a degrading server, adjusting network configurations to avoid bottlenecks, or even automatically patching software vulnerabilities before they can be exploited. This shift from reactive response to proactive prevention significantly enhances system uptime and reduces the likelihood of service disruptions.

The vision of fully autonomous systems is also rapidly becoming a tangible reality. These platforms will possess the intelligence to automatically optimize their configurations in response to real-time conditions, dynamically scaling resources up or down based on predicted demand patterns. In the event of a component failure, they will be able to reroute traffic around the affected area, ensuring continuous service availability. Furthermore, advanced AI algorithms will enable these systems to self-diagnose certain types of failures, identify the root causes, and initiate automated repair procedures, often without any human intervention. This could involve automatically restarting failed services, reallocating storage resources, or even rolling back problematic software deployments.

The ability of these future systems to learn from past incidents and automatically adapt their behavior is a crucial aspect of their enhanced resilience. By analyzing the root causes of previous failures and the effectiveness of past recovery actions, AI-powered platforms can refine their prediction models, optimize their remediation strategies, and even proactively adjust their configurations to prevent similar incidents from occurring in the future. This continuous learning loop will lead to increasingly robust and self-optimizing data architectures that become more resilient over time.

Designing for fault tolerance and resilience in the age of petabyte-scale data transcends the mere mitigation of negative impacts; it is about architecting systems that are inherently more robust, consistently reliable, and ultimately, deliver greater and more continuous value. By wholeheartedly embracing the inevitability of failure as a fundamental design constraint and by diligently applying the principles and established patterns of redundancy, isolation, self-healing, and proactive monitoring, organizations can construct data platforms that are not only capable of surviving the immense challenges of operating at massive scale but also possess the inherent strength to thrive in the face of adversity.

The ongoing journey towards building truly resilient systems is a dynamic process, characterized by continuous learning, constant adaptation, and an unwavering commitment to improvement. As we move towards increasingly intelligent and autonomous architectures, the ability to predict, prevent, and autonomously recover from failures will become the hallmark of next-generation data platforms. These systems will not just survive; they will learn, adapt, and ultimately flourish, ensuring the continuous availability, unwavering integrity, and uninterrupted delivery of critical services in a world increasingly reliant on the insights derived from vast oceans of data. The future of petabyte-scale data management lies in embracing intelligent resilience, building systems that not only withstand the storm but emerge stronger and more capable on the other side.

CHAPTER FOUR

DATA INGESTION AT SCALE

In the world of big data, ingestion is the first and arguably most critical step in the data pipeline. Before data can be processed, analyzed, or visualized, it must first be collected and transported often from a vast array of sources into a centralized system. As enterprises increasingly rely on real-time decision-making and insights drawn from massive volumes of data, the importance of scaling data ingestion infrastructure cannot be overstated. This chapter dives into the complexities of ingesting petabytes of data efficiently and reliably, highlighting architectural decisions, tools, and strategies required to build robust ingestion systems.

The Challenge of Ingesting at Petabyte Scale

The challenge of ingesting data at the petabyte scale transcends the rudimentary act of simply accommodating colossal datasets or managing torrents of high-velocity information. It metamorphoses into a profoundly intricate endeavor, demanding the meticulous orchestration of highly distributed systems that must perform the critical functions of data collection, reliable transportation, and rigorous validation across a heterogeneous landscape of data origins. These sources frequently span vast geographical distances, residing within the confines of private data centers and the fluid boundaries of hybrid cloud environments, each presenting its own unique set of connectivity constraints and data characteristics. Building an effective ingestion layer at this scale necessitates not merely the application of brute-force scaling techniques but the intelligent and thoughtful design of inherently robust and remarkably adaptable architectures, capable of gracefully navigating a labyrinth of inherent complexities and a multitude of potential operational pitfalls.

At this monumental echelon of data volume, the ingestion layer ceases to be a mere conduit for data entry; it transforms into a potentially critical bottleneck that can severely impede the efficiency and overall performance of the entire data pipeline if not architected with exceptional foresight and precision. This initial point of contact with the raw data must possess an intrinsic and deeply embedded resilience to the inevitable spectrum of failures that are endemic to large-scale distributed systems. These include the unpredictable fragmentation of network connectivity (network partitions), the transient or permanent outage of individual processing nodes within the ingestion cluster, and a myriad of other transient service disruptions that can occur in complex, interconnected environments. The underlying architecture must proactively anticipate these potential points of failure and seamlessly incorporate robust mechanisms for automatic retries of failed data transfers, intelligent message buffering to absorb temporary backpressure and prevent data loss during transient outages, and strategic data replication to ensure data durability even if individual ingestion nodes experience failures. Without these foundational resilience mechanisms, the integrity and completeness of the ingested data are perpetually at risk.

Furthermore, the ingestion layer must exhibit an exceptional degree of agility and flexibility in its capacity to seamlessly integrate with and effectively process an extraordinarily diverse spectrum of data formats. This data heterogeneity can range from meticulously structured relational datasets originating from traditional databases and well-defined transactional systems, to a plethora of semi-structured formats such as the key-value pairs of JSON and the tagged hierarchies of XML commonly found in API responses and configuration files, and extending to the inherently complex and often schema-less realm of completely unstructured data, encompassing vast repositories of textual documents, high-resolution imagery, and voluminous streams of video and audio content. Each of these disparate data formats presents its own unique set of parsing requirements, validation rules, and potential encoding challenges, demanding an ingestion pipeline that is not only versatile in its format support but also highly adaptable in its processing logic. The ability to dynamically interpret and validate data based on its inherent structure or lack thereof is paramount to ensuring data quality from the very outset.

The imperative for extreme scalability is a non-negotiable requirement at the petabyte scale. The underlying architecture must be designed with the inherent capability to dynamically accommodate not only the consistently growing volumes of data being generated but also the often unpredictable and highly variable fluctuations in ingestion workloads. This necessitates the strategic leveraging of horizontally scalable technologies, which can distribute the computational and network burden of data ingestion across a large and potentially elastic cluster of commodity hardware resources, or the intelligent utilization of the on-demand scaling capabilities offered by specialized cloud-based data ingestion services. The ability to automatically and seamlessly scale up the ingestion capacity during periods of peak data arrival or intensive batch loading, and equally importantly, to automatically scale down during periods of lower activity to optimize resource utilization and minimize operational costs, is a critical characteristic of a well-designed petabyte-scale ingestion system.

Critically, at this immense scale of data and infrastructure, even seemingly minor architectural inefficiencies, which might have been negligible in smaller deployments, can be dramatically amplified, leading to significant performance bottlenecks that ripple throughout the entire data pipeline, substantial increases in operational expenditures, and potentially unacceptable delays in making data available for downstream processing and analytical consumption. A suboptimal choice in data serialization format (e.g., using a verbose format when a more compact one would suffice), an inefficient data routing strategy that leads to unnecessary network hops and bandwidth contention, or a lack of intelligent data partitioning that results in uneven workload distribution across ingestion nodes can all have cascading and detrimental effects. Therefore, the fundamental architectural choices made at the ingestion layer become a crucial and often defining factor in the overall performance and sustainability of the entire data platform, influencing everything from the speed at which raw data is transformed into actionable insights to the total cost of ownership of the underlying data infrastructure. The design philosophy must prioritize the minimization of unnecessary data movement across the network, the optimization of data transformations as close to the data source as feasible (edge processing), and the meticulous orchestration of resource utilization across the distributed ingestion infrastructure to ensure maximum efficiency and cost-effectiveness.

Batch Ingestion vs. Streaming Ingestion

Batch ingestion operates on the principle of accumulating data over a predefined temporal window, which can range from minutes to hours or even days, and subsequently processing this collected data as a discrete, finite unit or "batch."

This approach typically involves scheduling periodic jobs that extract data from source systems, transform it into a desired format, and load it into a target data store. Batch processing is often simpler to conceptualize and implement, leveraging well-established Extract, Transform, Load (ETL) methodologies and tools. It proves particularly well-suited for scenarios where near-real-time data updates are not a critical requirement. Classic examples include nightly ETL pipelines that consolidate transactional data for business intelligence reporting, the periodic loading of historical customer profiles from CRM systems for trend analysis, or the bulk ingestion of log files for security auditing conducted at regular intervals. The inherent nature of batch processing allows for more extensive data transformations and aggregations to be performed before the data is made available for consumption, and it can often be more tolerant of transient network issues as the entire batch can be retried if necessary. However, the inherent latency introduced by the data collection period means that insights derived from batch-processed data are inherently delayed, reflecting the state of the data at the end of the collection window.

Streaming Ingestion: The Continuous Flow of Insights

In stark contrast, streaming ingestion adopts a paradigm where data flows continuously from its point of origin to its ultimate destination, enabling near-instantaneous processing and analysis of individual data events as they occur. This approach necessitates the establishment of persistent connections and the utilization of message brokers or stream processing platforms that can handle a continuous torrent of data. Streaming ingestion is absolutely essential for a growing number of modern applications that demand immediate insights and real-time decision-making capabilities. Critical use cases include real-time fraud detection systems that analyze transactional data as it happens to identify and prevent fraudulent activities, real-time personalization engines that adapt recommendations and user experiences based on immediate user interactions, predictive maintenance applications that analyze sensor data from industrial equipment in real-time to detect anomalies indicative of impending failures, and real-time monitoring dashboards that provide up-to-the-second visibility into key performance indicators. Streaming systems inherently introduce a higher degree of architectural complexity compared to batch systems. They must be designed to handle data arriving in an unpredictable order, ensure data consistency across distributed processing nodes, and implement robust error handling mechanisms to deal with individual event processing failures without interrupting the continuous flow of data. Furthermore, maintaining data ordering and providing exactly once processing guarantees in a distributed streaming environment presents significant technical challenges that require sophisticated coordination and state management.

The Blended Reality: Hybrid Architectures

Recognizing the distinct strengths and weaknesses of both batch and streaming ingestion, hybrid architectures are becoming increasingly prevalent in modern data platforms. These hybrid approaches strategically blend batch and streaming methodologies to leverage the advantages of each, catering to a wider range of analytical and operational needs. A common example is a real-time operational dashboard that relies on continuously ingested streaming data to display up-to-the-second metrics and alerts, while simultaneously utilizing batch-processed historical data to provide valuable contextual information, trend analysis, and comparative baselines. Another scenario might involve using a streaming pipeline for immediate anomaly detection and alerting, while periodically batch-processing the same data for more comprehensive forensic analysis and model retraining. The design of hybrid architectures requires careful consideration of data synchronization between the batch and streaming layers, ensuring consistency and providing a unified view of the data across different temporal granularities. These hybrid models offer a pragmatic approach to balancing the low latency and real-time insights of streaming with the simplicity and analytical depth often associated with batch processing, ultimately providing a more comprehensive and versatile data processing capability.

Message Queues: The Backbone of Real-Time Ingestion

At the very core of numerous highly scalable and resilient data ingestion systems lies the indispensable technology of distributed message queues, exemplified by robust platforms such as Apache Kafka and Apache Pulsar. These sophisticated publish-subscribe systems serve as the critical intermediary layer, elegantly decoupling the entities that produce data from the diverse array of consumers that subsequently process and analyze this information. This fundamental decoupling provides a multitude of architectural advantages, most notably enabling ingestion systems to absorb and manage data at exceptionally high throughput rates without overwhelming the downstream processing components. By acting as a robust buffer and providing a stable intermediary point, message queues ensure that the pace of data generation, which can often be unpredictable and subject to sudden surges, does not directly dictate the processing capacity of the consuming systems, thereby preventing system instability and data loss.

Apache Kafka The Durable and High-Performance Event Backbone

Apache Kafka has emerged as a dominant force in the realm of distributed message queues, renowned for its exceptional durability, remarkable performance characteristics, and inherent scalability. Kafka organizes streams of related messages into logical units known as "topics." Each topic is further subdivided into ordered; immutable sequences of records called "partitions." This partitioning mechanism is crucial for achieving horizontal scalability, as individual partitions can be distributed across multiple broker nodes within the Kafka cluster, allowing for parallel processing and increased throughput. Kafka's design emphasizes durability through its commit log, ensuring that messages persisted on disk across multiple brokers based on configurable replication factors, thus providing strong guarantees against data loss even in the face of broker failures. Furthermore, Kafka's architecture is optimized for high throughput read and write operations, making it capable of handling massive volumes of real-time data with low latency. Its inherent replay capabilities, allowing consumers to rewind and re-consume historical messages, are invaluable for scenarios requiring reprocessing of data due to errors or the deployment of new analytical models. Moreover, Kafka's seamless integration with powerful stream processing frameworks such as Apache Flink and Kafka Streams positions it as a cornerstone of modern event-driven architectures, enabling the development of sophisticated real-time data processing pipelines directly on the message streams.

Apache Pulsar Architectural Distinctions for Complex Deployments

Apache Pulsar, while sharing the fundamental concepts of a distributed publish-subscribe messaging system with Kafka, offers some notable architectural distinctions that make it particularly appealing in complex and geographically distributed deployments. One key difference lies in its separation of the serving (brokers) and storage (bookies) layers. Brokers are stateless and responsible for serving read and write requests, while the actual data storage is handled by a separate, durable storage layer based on Apache Bookkeeper. This separation allows for independent scaling of the serving and storage capacities, providing greater flexibility in resource management and cost optimization, especially in scenarios with varying read/write ratios and storage requirements. Pulsar also provides native, built-in support for multi-tenancy, enabling multiple independent tenants to securely share the same Pulsar cluster with strong isolation guarantees. Its robust geo-replication capabilities, allowing for seamless replication of messages across multiple geographically dispersed data centers, make it a compelling choice for applications requiring high availability and disaster recovery across multiple regions. Additionally, Pulsar offers a unified platform that supports both traditional message queuing semantics (with features like message acknowledgments and guaranteed delivery) and stream processing functionalities through its "Pulsar Functions" framework, providing development teams with greater flexibility in choosing the most appropriate processing paradigm for their specific use cases.

Message Queues as Elastic Buffers: Absorbing Data Spikes

Beyond their role in decoupling producers and consumers and enabling horizontal scalability, message queues also serve as invaluable elastic buffers that can effectively absorb transient spikes in data volume. During periods of unusually high data generation rates, which are common in real-world systems due to various events or peak usage times, the message queue acts as a temporary holding area for the incoming data. This buffering mechanism prevents downstream processing systems, which may have a more limited processing capacity or experience temporary slowdowns due to resource constraints or transient issues, from being overwhelmed by the sudden influx of data. The message queue ensures that the data is not lost during these periods of high load, allowing downstream consumers to process the backlog of messages at their own pace once the data generation rate subsides or their processing capacity recovers. This inherent buffering capability is crucial for maintaining the stability and reliability of the entire ingestion pipeline, ensuring that temporary slowdowns in one part of the system do not lead to catastrophic data loss or system-wide failures. The configurable retention policies of message queues also provide a mechanism to store data for a defined period, allowing consumers to recover and reprocess data in case of failures or the need for historical analysis.

Handling Backpressure in Ingestion Pipelines

In the dynamic and often unpredictable world of petabyte-scale data ingestion, a critical challenge arises when the rate at which data is produced significantly outpaces the capacity of downstream systems to consume and process it. This phenomenon, known as **backpressure**, poses a serious threat to the stability and reliability of ingestion pipelines. If not proactively and effectively managed, backpressure can lead to a cascade of detrimental consequences, including catastrophic system crashes due to resource exhaustion (memory overflows, disk full errors), irretrievable data loss as buffers overflow and new data is discarded, and severe processing delays that render real-time or near-real-time data pipelines effectively useless. To mitigate these risks and ensure the smooth and stable operation of high-throughput ingestion systems, a suite of sophisticated mechanisms are employed, encompassing flow control, rate limiting, intelligent buffering strategies, and controlled load shedding techniques.

Orchestrating the Flow: Flow Control Mechanisms for Cooperative Data Exchange

Flow control mechanisms provide a means for consumers to communicate their processing capacity and limitations back to the producers, enabling a more coordinated and balanced exchange of data. Reactive programming paradigms, with their emphasis on asynchronous data streams and the propagation of demand signals, offer powerful tools for implementing flow control. In these systems, consumers explicitly signal their readiness to process a certain amount of data, and producers respond by emitting data at a rate that aligns with this expressed demand. This cooperative approach prevents producers from overwhelming consumers and ensures that data is only sent when the receiving end is prepared to handle it. Techniques like acknowledgments and negative acknowledgments (NACKs) can be used to manage the reliable delivery and processing of data within these flow-controlled streams.

The Strategic Reservoir: Buffering for Burst Absorption and Smoothing

Buffering is another indispensable technique for managing backpressure in ingestion pipelines. It involves the temporary storage of incoming data, either in memory or on persistent disk, to act as a shock absorber for transient bursts in data production. When the rate of incoming data momentarily exceeds the processing capacity of downstream systems, the buffer acts as a temporary holding area, preventing data loss and allowing the consuming systems to catch up once the surge subsides. The size and characteristics of these buffers are critical design considerations. While larger buffers can accommodate longer or more intense bursts, they also introduce increased latency and can themselves become a point of failure if they overflow. Intelligent buffer management strategies often involve dynamic sizing, prioritization of certain data streams, and mechanisms for alerting when buffer utilization reaches critical thresholds.

Upstream Signals: Propagating Backpressure in Streaming Architectures

In modern stream processing systems, such as Apache Flink and Akka Streams, backpressure management is often handled through the elegant mechanism of propagating backpressure signals upstream towards the data producers. When a stream processing operator or a sink is experiencing processing bottlenecks and cannot keep up with the incoming data rate, it sends a signal back to the upstream operators, effectively instructing them to slow down the rate at which they are emitting data. This backpropagation of backpressure signals can traverse the entire processing topology, ultimately reaching the original data sources and throttling the rate of data production at its origin. This fine-grained control over the data flow ensures that processing stages are not overwhelmed, preventing resource exhaustion and maintaining the overall stability of the streaming pipeline. This approach requires careful coordination and communication between the different components of the streaming system.

The Necessary Sacrifice: Load Shedding in Extreme Overload Scenarios

In extreme backpressure scenarios where even flow control and buffering mechanisms are insufficient to cope with the overwhelming volume of incoming data, a last-resort technique known as load shedding may be employed. Load shedding involves the deliberate discarding of some incoming data to prevent catastrophic system failure. This is a trade-off that prioritizes the overall health and stability of the system over the completeness of the data. Implementing load shedding requires careful consideration of which data to discard (e.g., less critical data, older data) and the mechanisms for doing so in a controlled and informative manner. Strategies like sampling or dropping data based on certain criteria can be used to manage the data loss in a way that minimizes the impact on critical downstream processes.

The Delicate Equilibrium: Balancing Buffer Size, Latency, and Fault Tolerance

In high-throughput ingestion environments operating at petabyte scale, striking a delicate balance between buffer sizes, processing latency, and fault tolerance is a critical engineering challenge. Larger buffers can provide greater resilience to data bursts but introduce higher latency as data spends more time in transit. Conversely, smaller buffers can minimize latency but increase the risk of data loss during surges. The choice of buffer sizes must also consider the fault tolerance characteristics of the system. In the event of a failure, data held in volatile memory buffers may be lost, necessitating mechanisms for persistent buffering or reliable message delivery guarantees from the underlying messaging infrastructure. Therefore, the design of backpressure handling mechanisms requires a thorough understanding of the data production patterns, the processing capabilities of downstream systems, the desired latency characteristics of the pipeline, and the overall fault tolerance requirements of the application. Continuous monitoring and adaptive tuning of these parameters are often necessary to maintain optimal performance and stability in the face of evolving data loads and system conditions.

Schema Evolution and Data Format Flexibility

In the complex tapestry of petabyte-scale data ingestion, particularly when dealing with data streams originating from a multitude of producers potentially numbering in the thousands and often under the independent stewardship of diverse internal teams or external third-party entities the challenge of schema evolution emerges as a critical and potentially disruptive concern. A schema, serving as the blueprint for data structure, meticulously defines the constituent fields, their corresponding data types, and the intricate relationships that bind them together. Over time, these schemas are rarely static; they inevitably undergo modifications driven by evolving business requirements, the introduction of new features in source applications, or the integration of data from novel sources. Changes in schema, such as the addition of a new data field, the renaming of an existing one, or alterations to the underlying data types, can have severe and cascading consequences on downstream data consumers if not managed with meticulous care and a well-defined strategy. Unanticipated schema changes can lead to parsing errors, data type mismatches, incorrect data interpretations, and ultimately, the complete breakage of critical analytical pipelines and data-dependent applications.

To effectively address the complexities of schema evolution in such dynamic environments, the adoption of a schema registry is paramount. These centralized services, such as Confluent's Schema Registry (tightly integrated with Apache Kafka) or the built-in schema management capabilities offered by Apache Pulsar, provide a unified and authoritative repository for managing and validating the schemas associated with data streams. Producers register the schemes they intend to use for publishing data, and consumers can then retrieve these schemes to understand the structure of the incoming data. A key function of schema registries is the enforcement of schema compatibility rules. These rules, which can be configured to adhere to backward compatibility (new producer schemas can be read by older consumers), forward compatibility (older producer schemas can be read by newer consumers), or full compatibility (new and old schemas are mutually readable), provide a contract between data producers and consumers. By validating schema changes against these compatibility rules, the registry acts as a gatekeeper, preventing the introduction of schema modifications that would lead to unexpected failures or data corruption in consuming applications. This centralized control over schema evolution ensures a more stable and predictable data ecosystem.

The choice of serialization format also plays a significant role in facilitating schema evolution and ensuring data format flexibility. Formats like Avro, Protocol Buffers (Protobuf), and even JSON, while widely used, offer varying degrees of inherent support for schema evolution. Avro, in particular, is often favored in large-scale data ingestion scenarios due to its robust support for schema evolution and its ability to provide compact binary encoding, which optimizes network bandwidth and storage utilization. Avro achieves schema evolution by explicitly including the schema definition (or a schema identifier that allows retrieval from a schema registry) within each serialized message. When a consumer reads an Avro message, it uses its own version of the schema to interpret the data. Avro's resolution rules allow for graceful handling of differences between the producer's schema and the consumer's schema, such as the presence or absence of fields (with default values), or changes in field order. By embedding schema identifiers in the messages and performing schema validation at runtime, systems can evolve their data formats without requiring widespread downtime or extensive code rewrites in either producer or consumer applications.

Ensuring Data Consistency from a Multitude of Origins

In the sprawling landscape of large-scale ingestion systems, data can originate from tens of thousands of diverse sources ranging from individual IoT devices and ephemeral microservices to complex enterprise applications and external partner integrations ensuring data consistency presents a formidable challenge, particularly within the context of eventual consistency models that prioritize availability and partition tolerance over immediate consistency. The raw data ingested from these disparate sources often requires rigorous validation to ensure adherence to expected formats and data types, thorough deduplication to eliminate redundant records arising from retries or multiple data streams, and often enrichment with contextual information from other data sources to enhance its analytical value.

Idempotent Writes: The Cornerstone of Consistent Data Handling

Idempotent writes emerge as a crucial strategy in the pursuit of data consistency in such complex environments. An operation is considered idempotent if its repeated execution with the same input produces the same outcome as a single execution, without any unintended side effects. By designing ingestion pipelines and downstream storage mechanisms to support idempotent writes, systems can gracefully recover from network retries, partial failures during data transmission, and duplicate message deliveries without the risk of creating duplicate data records or introducing inconsistencies. This is often achieved by assigning unique identifiers to each data event at the source and ensuring that the processing logic at the ingestion and storage layers uses these identifiers to detect and handle duplicate attempts to write the same data.

Watermarking and Event-Time Processing: Reasoning About Time in Distributed Streams

Another vital strategy for ensuring data consistency, particularly in asynchronous and distributed streaming systems, involves the concepts of watermarking and event-time processing. Due to inherent network latencies, the distributed nature of data sources, and the partitioning of data streams for parallel processing, messages often arrive at the processing engine out of their original chronological order. Watermarks are a mechanism used to provide an estimate of the completeness of event-time data within a given time window. By tracking the observed event times and incorporating an allowable delay, systems can generate watermarks that signal when it is reasonably safe to assume that all events within a certain time range have arrived. This allows for accurate windowing, aggregation, and other time-based operations to be performed even on out-of-order data. Event-time processing, in contrast to processing based on system arrival time, uses the timestamp embedded within the data event itself to determine its position in the temporal sequence, providing a more accurate representation of the data's actual occurrence.

Distributed Tracing and Observability: Illuminating the Data's Journey

Finally, comprehensively distributed tracing and robust observability tools play an indispensable role in ensuring data consistency across large-scale ingestion systems. By tagging individual data events with unique identifiers as close to their origin as possible and then tracking their journey as they traverse various services and processing stages within the ingestion pipeline, teams gain end-to-end visibility into the flow of data. Distributed tracing allows for the identification and diagnosis of issues related to data corruption, unexpected delays in processing, or mismatches in data transformations between different components. Observability platforms that aggregate logs, metrics, and traces provide a holistic view of the system's health and performance, enabling rapid detection and resolution of anomalies that could potentially lead to data inconsistencies. By providing this granular visibility into the data's lifecycle, these tools empower engineering teams to proactively monitor data consistency and quickly pinpoint and rectify any deviations from the expected behavior.

In the contemporary digital landscape, where organizations are increasingly reliant on the immediacy and dynamism of real-time data to inform their operational decision-making and shape their overarching business strategies, the data ingestion layer has ascended to a position of paramount importance. It forms the very foundation upon which any modern and effective data platform is constructed. This critical layer is no longer merely a mechanism for transferring data; it must embody robustness to withstand the inherent challenges of distributed systems, exhibit exceptional flexibility to accommodate the ever-expanding diversity of data sources and formats, and possess intrinsic fault tolerance to ensure uninterrupted data flow even in the face of inevitable infrastructure anomalies.

The fundamental choices made in designing the ingestion layer, such as the strategic selection between batch and streaming methodologies to align with specific latency requirements and processing paradigms, the critical selection of the appropriate message queuing technology to provide decoupling and scalability, and the implementation of robust mechanisms for managing the complexities of schema evolution across a multitude of data producers, all have profound and far-reaching implications that reverberate throughout the entirety of the downstream data stack. Furthermore, the implementation of stringent data integrity measures, particularly in the face of eventual consistency models necessitated by distributed architectures and the sheer scale of data origins, is a non-negotiable requirement for building trust and confidence in the data being consumed.

Ultimately, the overarching goal in architecting a scalable data ingestion system is to create a robust and adaptable framework that not only possesses the inherent capacity to scale linearly and efficiently with the ever-increasing volume of data being generated but also demonstrates the agility to evolve in tandem with the growing complexity of the underlying business operations and analytical requirements. As the characteristics of data itself continue to expand along the dimensions of velocity (the speed at which data is generated), variety (the multitude of data formats and structures), and volume (the sheer quantity of data), the data ingestion system must possess the intrinsic capability to seamlessly adapt and meet these escalating demands – all without compromising the fundamental pillars of system reliability (ensuring consistent and dependable operation), data consistency (maintaining accuracy and integrity across the data landscape), or overall system performance (delivering timely and efficient data delivery).

The success of a modern data platform hinges critically on the effectiveness and scalability of its ingestion layer. A well-designed ingestion architecture acts as a stable and reliable on-ramp for data, ensuring a continuous and high-quality flow of information that fuels downstream analytics, powers real-time applications, and ultimately drives informed business decisions. Conversely, a poorly designed or inadequately scalable ingestion layer can become a significant bottleneck, hindering the organization's ability to leverage the full potential of its data assets and impeding its agility in responding to the rapidly evolving demands of the modern business environment. Therefore, meticulous planning, careful technology selection, and a deep understanding of the inherent challenges of data at scale are paramount in building a scalable data ingestion foundation that can effectively support the data-driven aspirations of any forward-thinking organization.

CHAPTER FIVE

STORAGE SOLUTIONS FOR MASSIVE DATASETS

The preceding chapters have meticulously laid the groundwork, highlighting the multifaceted challenges and intricate architectural considerations that arise when organizations grapple with the sheer scale and complexity of petabyte-level data. At the heart of any successful strategy for managing such colossal volumes lies the critical decision of selecting and implementing appropriate storage solutions. It is an undeniable truth that not all storage systems are created equal, particularly when confronted with the unique demands of petabyte-scale data – encompassing not only immense capacity but also the need for high throughput, diverse data format support, varying access patterns, and stringent cost efficiency. This chapter embarks on an exhaustive exploration of the prominent storage paradigms that have emerged to tackle these monumental challenges. We will conduct a detailed comparative analysis of distributed file systems, exemplified by the foundational Hadoop Distributed File System (HDFS) and the ubiquitous Amazon Simple Storage Service (S3), the expansive and versatile landscape of NoSQL databases, with a specific focus on the characteristics of Cassandra and Google Bigtable, and the conceptual distinct yet increasingly convergent domains of data lakes and traditional data warehouses. Furthermore, we will delve into the strategic and tactical considerations surrounding the implementation of tiered storage architectures, meticulously examining the optimization of hot, warm, and cold storage tiers to achieve a delicate and cost-effective equilibrium between performance accessibility and economic realities across the varying stages of data lifecycle and the diverse patterns of data access.

Navigating the Petabyte Storage Maze: A Landscape of Diverse Solutions

The relentless deluge of data, fueled by advancements in IoT, AI/ML, scientific research, and digital transformation initiatives, has propelled organizations into the daunting realm of petabyte-scale storage. Within this ever-expanding labyrinth of information, the limitations of traditional, monolithic storage solutions become starkly apparent. These legacy systems, often characterized by their centralized nature, reliance on single points of scaling (typically vertical expansion through expensive hardware upgrades), and proprietary architectures, invariably buckle under the immense strain of capacity constraints. They encounter significant performance bottlenecks when handling massive concurrent access from diverse applications and users, and frequently present unsustainable cost models for storing such vast quantities of information, often involving vendor lock-in and exorbitant scaling costs.

The imperative for adopting distributed and inherently scalable storage architectures becomes not merely a strategic recommendation but a fundamental necessity for organizational survival and the attainment of a crucial competitive advantage in this data-driven era. The ability to efficiently store, manage, and analyze petabytes of data unlocks unprecedented insights, fuels innovation, and enables organizations to respond agilely to evolving market dynamics. Conversely, being constrained by outdated storage infrastructure can cripple operational efficiency, stifle innovation, and ultimately lead to a competitive disadvantage.

This chapter will serve as a comprehensive guide through the key categories of storage solutions that have emerged as frontrunners in addressing these formidable challenges. We will meticulously dissect their core architectural principles, delving into the underlying mechanisms that enable their scalability and performance. We will highlight their intrinsic strengths, meticulously outlining the specific use cases and data characteristics where they excel. Conversely, we will also address their inherent weaknesses and potential limitations, providing a balanced perspective for informed decision-making. Ultimately, this chapter aims to provide a robust framework for understanding the nuanced suitability of each solution for accommodating different types of massive datasets, supporting a wide spectrum of analytical workloads, and aligning with varying organizational needs and budgetary constraints within the complex landscape of petabyte-scale storage. We will explore the following key categories in detail:

1. Distributed File Systems (Scale-Out NAS):

Core Architectural Principles: We will delve into the distributed nature of these systems, examining how data is spread across multiple nodes, often leveraging commodity hardware. We will explore concepts like parallel access, data striping, and distributed metadata management that contribute to their scalability and performance. Different consistency models and their implications for data access will also be discussed.

Strengths: We will highlight their ease of integration with existing file-based applications, their ability to scale capacity and performance independently, and their often-simplified management compared to more complex distributed systems. We will explore their suitability for unstructured and semi-structured data, large file repositories, and collaborative workflows.

Weaknesses: We will analyze potential limitations in handling very small files or highly transactional workloads, as well as the potential for increased latency compared to block-based storage in certain scenarios. We will also discuss the trade-offs associated with different consistency models.

2. Object Storage:

Core Architectural Principles: We will dissect the fundamental concept of storing data as objects within a flat address space, eliminating the hierarchical file system structure. We will explore key characteristics like metadata association with objects, RESTful APIs for access, and the inherent scalability and durability offered by distributed architectures. We will also discuss different storage classes and their implications for cost and access latency.

Strengths: We will emphasize their exceptional scalability and cost-effectiveness for storing massive amounts of unstructured data, their robust durability and availability features, and their seamless integration with cloud-native applications and data lakes. We will explore use cases like archiving, content delivery, big data analytics, and AI/ML training datasets.

Weaknesses: We will analyze their limitations in directly supporting traditional file system semantics and the potential need for application-level modifications to leverage object storage effectively. We will also discuss performance considerations for random access patterns and transactional workloads.

3. Distributed Block Storage (Software-Defined Storage):

Core Architectural Principles: We will explore how software-defined storage solutions abstract the underlying hardware, enabling the creation of highly scalable and resilient block storage pools from commodity hardware. We will delve into concepts like data replication, erasure coding, and distributed volume management that ensure data availability and performance. We will also discuss different software-defined storage architectures and their varying characteristics.

Strengths: We will highlight their ability to provide high-performance block-level access for demanding applications like databases and virtualized environments, their flexibility in scaling capacity and performance independently, and their potential for cost savings compared to traditional SANs. We will explore their suitability for mission-critical applications requiring low latency and high throughput.

Weaknesses: We will analyze the potential complexity in initial setup and ongoing management, as well as the performance variability that can arise depending on the underlying hardware and software configuration. We will also discuss the importance of careful resource planning and performance tuning.

4. Hyperscale Cloud Storage:

Core Architectural Principles: We will examine the massively scalable and globally distributed storage services offered by major cloud providers. We will explore their pay-as-you-go pricing models, their diverse range of storage tiers optimized for different access patterns and cost sensitivities, and their integrated services for data management, analytics, and security.

Strengths: We will emphasize their unparalleled scalability and elasticity, their operational simplicity with managed services, their global accessibility, and their rich ecosystem of integrated cloud services. We will explore their suitability for a wide range of workloads, from archival to high-performance computing and big data analytics.

Weaknesses: We will analyze potential concerns around data sovereignty, vendor lock-in, egress fees, and the need for robust network connectivity. We will also discuss the importance of careful cost optimization and security configuration in cloud environments.

By meticulously examining these diverse storage solutions, this chapter aims to equip organizations with the knowledge necessary to navigate the petabyte storage maze effectively. Understanding the core principles, strengths, and weaknesses of each approach will empower them to make informed decisions aligned with their specific data characteristics, performance requirements, analytical workloads, budgetary constraints, and long-term strategic goals in the era of exponentially growing data.

Distributed File Systems: The Bedrock of Scalable Data Processing and Cost-Effective Storage

Distributed file systems, with prominent examples like the Hadoop Distributed File System (HDFS) and Amazon Simple Storage Service (S3), have fundamentally reshaped the landscape of data storage and processing for organizations grappling with the challenges of petabyte-scale datasets. These systems represent a paradigm shift from traditional monolithic storage, offering horizontal scalability, fault tolerance, and cost-effectiveness that are crucial for managing and deriving value from massive volumes of information.

HDFS, a cornerstone of the open-source Apache Hadoop ecosystem, emerged as a revolutionary solution specifically engineered to address the limitations of traditional file systems when dealing with truly massive datasets. Its core design principle revolves around the ability to operate efficiently and reliably on clusters of commodity-grade hardware. This deliberate choice democratized big data storage, allowing organizations to scale horizontally by adding more inexpensive servers rather than relying on costly, proprietary upgrades.

The architecture of HDFS inherently provides a fault-tolerant and high-throughput storage layer that is particularly well-suited for the sequential read and write patterns characteristic of batch processing workloads. This focus on sequential operations aligns perfectly with the MapReduce paradigm, where large datasets are processed in parallel through a series of map and reduce tasks.

HDFS achieves its remarkable scalability by distributing vast datasets across a multitude of interconnected nodes within a cluster. Data is broken down into large blocks (typically 128MB by default) and these blocks are spread across different DataNodes. To ensure both data durability in the face of inevitable hardware failures and high availability for data access, HDFS employs data redundancy, with triple replication being the default configuration. This means each data block is typically stored on three different DataNodes, ensuring that the loss of one or even two nodes will not result in data loss or service interruption. The NameNode acts as the central metadata manager, maintaining the namespace of the file system and the mapping of data blocks to DataNodes. While the NameNode itself can be a single point of failure (addressed through High Availability configurations), the distributed nature of the DataNodes provides robust resilience for the actual data storage.

In contrast to HDFS's on-premise or self-managed nature, Amazon S3 is a highly scalable object storage service offered within the Amazon Web Services (AWS) cloud infrastructure. It represents a different architectural approach, focusing on storing data as objects with associated metadata in a flat address space. S3 boasts virtually unlimited storage capacity, dynamically scaling to accommodate growing data needs without requiring manual intervention or capacity planning.

One of S3's most compelling features is its industry-leading data durability, often cited as "eleven nines" (99.999999999%), which translates to an extremely low probability of data loss over a given year. This exceptional durability is achieved through storing data across multiple Availability Zones (AZs) within an AWS Region. Furthermore, S3 offers a cost-effective pricing model based on storage usage, data transfer, and the number of requests, making it an exceptionally popular choice for a wide range of use cases.

S3 has become a foundational storage layer for building scalable data lakes, acting as a central repository for diverse data types in their raw or processed forms. Its robust durability and scalability make it an ideal choice for reliable archival repositories, ensuring long-term data preservation. Moreover, S3 seamlessly integrates with a wide array of cloud-based data processing frameworks, including Apache Spark on Amazon EMR (Elastic MapReduce), serverless compute services like AWS Lambda and AWS Glue, and various data analytics platforms. Its RESTful API allows for easy programmatic access and integration with a vast ecosystem of tools and applications.

Common Strengths and Key Considerations

Both HDFS and S3 excel at the efficient storage of large, often unstructured or semi-structured files, making them ideal for storing raw data, log files, media content, and other large datasets. They frequently serve as the primary storage substrate for big data processing engines like Spark and the traditional MapReduce paradigm, providing the necessary scale and throughput for distributed data analysis. Their ability to handle massive datasets and their inherent scalability are crucial for organizations looking to extract valuable insights from their ever-growing data assets.

Limitations and Suitability for Different Workloads

However, it is important to note that these distributed file systems are generally not optimized for scenarios demanding low-latency random access patterns or high-frequency transactional workloads. The architectural overhead associated with distributed coordination, metadata lookups, and file-based access can introduce significant performance limitations in such use cases. For instance, applications requiring frequent small reads or writes to random locations within files may experience high latency and low throughput on HDFS or S3 compared to block-based storage solutions. Similarly, transactional databases with stringent consistency and low-latency requirements are typically better suited for storage systems designed for random I/O and transactional integrity.

Distributed file systems like HDFS and S3 represent a critical evolution in data storage, providing the scalability, fault tolerance, and cost-effectiveness necessary to manage and process petabyte-scale datasets. While they excel at storing large files and supporting batch-oriented analytical workloads, their limitations in handling low-latency random access and high-frequency transactions necessitate the consideration of other specialized storage solutions for different types of data and application requirements. Understanding these nuances is crucial for designing efficient and performant data architectures in the era of big data.

NoSQL Databases: Embracing Flexibility, Scalability, and Diverse Data Models Beyond Relational Constraints

The advent and widespread adoption of NoSQL databases have provided a compelling array of alternative storage solutions that often prioritize horizontal scalability, high availability, and flexible data models over the rigid schemas and strong consistency guarantees traditionally associated with relational database management systems (RDBMS). This diverse category of databases encompasses a wide spectrum of data models, each with its own unique approach to organizing and querying data, thereby making them particularly well-suited for a variety of use cases involving massive datasets characterized by evolving schemas, high read and write throughput requirements, or non-relational data structures. Key-value stores, document databases, column-family stores, and graph databases each offer distinct advantages in terms of data organization and query capabilities, providing architects with a rich palette of options for addressing specific petabyte-scale storage challenges.

Cassandra, a prominent distributed NoSQL database employing a column-family data model, has garnered significant acclaim for its exceptional high availability and its ability to scale horizontally in a near-linear fashion. Its masterless, peer-to-peer architecture ensures remarkable resilience to individual node failures, as no single point of failure can bring down the entire cluster. Furthermore, Cassandra's architecture is highly optimized for handling massive volumes of write operations, making it an ideal choice for applications that involve continuous high-velocity data ingestion, such as storing time-series data from sensors, managing social media feeds with rapid updates, and handling high-throughput logging.

Google Bigtable, another influential NoSQL database, is a highly scalable and performant column-oriented data store specifically engineered to handle petabytes of both structured and semi-structured data. It underpins many of Google's core services, including Gmail, Google Maps, and YouTube, a testament to its ability to deliver low latency reads and writes even at extreme scale. Its column-family orientation allows for efficient storage and retrieval of sparse data, and its design prioritizes consistent performance under heavy load, making it a strong contender for real-time analytical applications and services with stringent performance requirements.

The broader NoSQL landscape presents a rich tapestry of choices beyond Cassandra and Bigtable, including document databases like MongoDB, key-value stores like Redis and Amazon DynamoDB, and graph databases like Neo4j. Each of these subcategories offers unique trade-offs in terms of consistency models (ranging from eventual consistency, which prioritizes availability and partition tolerance, to strong consistency, which prioritizes data accuracy across the distributed system), the degree of data modeling flexibility afforded to developers, and the specific query capabilities supported by the database. Selecting the most appropriate NoSQL database for a petabyte-scale application necessitates a thorough and nuanced understanding of the specific data access patterns anticipated, the criticality of data consistency for the use case, and the precise scalability and performance benchmarks that must be achieved.

The concepts of data lakes and traditional data warehouses represent two historically distinct yet increasingly converging paradigms for the storage and subsequent analysis of large volumes of data. Data lakes, typically constructed on top of highly scalable and cost-effective distributed object storage systems like S3, Azure Data Lake Storage, or Google Cloud Storage, are fundamentally designed to accommodate vast quantities of raw data in its native, often untransformed format. This includes structured data from relational databases, semi-structured data such as JSON and XML, and entirely unstructured data like text, images, and video. Data lakes embrace a "schema-on-read" philosophy, deferring the definition and application of data structure until the point of analysis. This inherent flexibility makes them exceptionally well-suited for exploratory data science initiatives, machine learning model development that often requires access to raw, granular data, and a wide range of diverse analytical workloads where the specific data requirements may evolve rapidly. The absence of rigid upfront schema enforcement allows for greater agility in ingesting and exploring new and varied data sources without the time-consuming and often restrictive process of upfront data modeling and transformation.

In contrast, traditional data warehouses have historically adhered to a "schema-on-write" approach, mandating that data be meticulously transformed, cleaned, and modeled into a predefined, structured format before it is loaded into the warehouse. These systems are primarily optimized for business intelligence (BI) and generating standardized reports, providing a consistent and well-governed repository of data for answering predefined business questions. Modern data warehouses, such as Snowflake, Google BigQuery, and Amazon Redshift, have evolved significantly to handle massive datasets and offer advanced features like columnar storage (which optimizes analytical query performance), Massively Parallel Processing (MPP) architectures for high-speed query execution, and sophisticated query optimizers.

The once clear distinction between data lakes and data warehouses is becoming increasingly blurred with the emergence and rapid adoption of "lakehouse" architectures. This innovative paradigm seeks to bridge the historical divide by combining the inherent flexibility and scalability of data lakes with the robust data management capabilities and performance querying traditionally associated with data warehouses. These lakehouse architectures often leverage open-source technologies like Apache Iceberg and Delta Lake, which introduce features such as ACID (Atomicity, Consistency, Isolation, Durability) transactions, robust schema evolution support, and data versioning directly onto data lake storage layers. This enables organizations to perform more reliable and performant analytical workloads, including complex SQL queries and data warehousing tasks, directly on the vast and flexible data lake, effectively unifying their data storage and analytical infrastructure.

Tiered Storage: Strategically Balancing Cost and Performance Across the Data Lifecycle

As data volumes burgeon into the petabyte scale, the economic realities of storing and accessing all of it at consistently high-performance levels can become prohibitively expensive. Tiered storage strategies offer a pragmatic and cost-effective solution by intelligently categorizing data based on its frequency of access and its associated performance requirements. Once categorized, data is then strategically stored on different types of storage media that offer varying trade-offs between cost and performance characteristics. A commonly adopted tiered storage model typically encompasses the following distinct tiers:

Hot Storage: This tier represents the highest-performance storage layer, often utilizing cutting-edge storage media such as Solid-State Drives (SSDs) or Non-Volatile Memory express (NVMe) drives. It is specifically designed to host data that is accessed frequently and demands the lowest possible latency for reading and writing operations. This tier is typically the most expensive on a per-unit basis but provides the crucial performance needed for critical, time-sensitive workloads and for accessing recent or actively analyzed datasets.

Warm Storage: Positioned as a middle ground, the warm storage tier aims to strike a balance between cost-effectiveness and acceptable performance. It often leverages high-capacity Hard Disk Drives (HDDs) or less expensive cloud-based storage options that offer reasonable read/write speeds. This tier is well-suited for data that is accessed less frequently than hot data but still needs to be readily available with moderate latency, such as data used for periodic reporting or analysis that doesn't have stringent real-time requirements.

Cold Storage: Prioritizing cost efficiency above all else, the cold storage tier is designed for data that is accessed infrequently or primarily intended for long-term archival purposes. It often utilizes technologies like magnetic tape libraries or deeply discounted, low-cost cloud archival storage services (such as AWS Glacier, Azure Archive Storage, or Google Cloud Archive). Accessing data residing in cold storage typically involves significantly higher latency and may incur retrieval costs, making it suitable for data that is rarely needed but must be retained for compliance or historical reasons.

Implementing a successful tiered storage strategy necessitates the definition of clear and well-articulated data lifecycle policies. These policies should automate the seamless migration of data between different storage tiers based on predefined criteria, such as the age of the data, its frequency of access, and its ongoing business value. This automated data movement ensures that frequently accessed, high-value data resides on the fastest (and often most expensive) storage, while less frequently accessed, lower-priority data is relegated to more cost-effective (but potentially slower) storage tiers. Effective implementation often relies on data management tools and the built-in lifecycle management features offered by cloud storage services, which can automate the tiering process based on user-defined rules. This strategic optimization of storage resources can lead to significant reductions in overall storage costs while simultaneously ensuring that performance-critical data remains on high-performance storage for optimal accessibility.

Strategically Architecting Storage for the Petabyte Era and Beyond

The strategic selection and meticulous implementation of storage solutions for massive datasets represent a critical architectural undertaking that directly and profoundly impacts system performance, overall cost efficiency, inherent scalability, and ultimately, the organization's ability to effectively harness the immense potential of its data for diverse analytical and operational endeavors. In the complex landscape of petabyte-scale data management, a monolithic or one-size-fits-all approach is rarely effective. The optimal storage strategy often involves a carefully considered combination of different storage paradigms, intelligently chosen and orchestrated to align precisely with the specific characteristics of the data being managed, the diverse requirements of the anticipated workloads, and the overarching strategic objectives of the business. A deep and nuanced understanding of the intrinsic strengths and inherent weaknesses of distributed file systems, the versatile landscape of NoSQL databases, the contrasting yet converging paradigms of data lakes and data warehouses, as well as the strategic and economic benefits of well-implemented tiered storage architectures, is absolutely essential for navigating the complexities of petabyte-scale data management and constructing a robust and cost-effective data platform that can adapt and evolve for the future. As the relentless growth of data continues its exponential trajectory, a thoughtful, adaptive, and strategically informed approach to storage architecture will serve as a key differentiator for organizations striving to unlock the full and transformative potential of their ever-expanding data assets.

CHAPTER SIX

EFFICIENT DATA PROCESSING FRAMEWORKS

Processing petabytes of information demands a paradigm shift from traditional, single-node processing to distributed frameworks that can harness the power of parallelism to tackle computationally intensive tasks and minimize the inherent latency associated with large-scale data manipulation. This chapter delves into the core of modern data processing engines, exploring prominent frameworks such as Apache Spark, Apache Flink, and Dask, each offering unique capabilities for handling massive datasets. We will also examine the burgeoning landscape of serverless compute options, exemplified by AWS Lambda, and their role in enabling event-driven data processing workflows. Furthermore, this chapter will cover critical optimization techniques, including strategic data partitioning, intelligent indexing, and the performance-enhancing power of vectorized execution, all essential for achieving efficiency and speed in petabyte-scale analytics.

The landscape of petabyte-scale analytics is dominated by several powerful data processing engines, each meticulously designed with unique architectural philosophies and optimized for specific types of workloads. Understanding the nuances of these engines is crucial for organizations seeking to effectively process and derive value from their massive datasets. Let's delve deeper into Apache Spark, Apache Flink, and Dask

Apache Spark: The Versatile Workhorse for Big Data

Apache Spark has emerged as a dominant force in the realm of big data processing, establishing itself as a unified engine capable of handling a diverse range of analytical tasks. Its strength lies in its ability to seamlessly integrate batch processing, stream processing, machine learning, graph processing, and SQL analytics within a single, cohesive framework. This versatility eliminates the need for disparate processing systems, simplifying data pipelines and reducing operational complexity.

At its core, Spark's innovation lies in its in-memory processing capabilities. By caching intermediate computation results in memory across distributed nodes, Spark can significantly accelerate iterative algorithms and data transformations that are common in many data science and machine learning workflows. This in-memory paradigm contrasts with earlier disk-based systems like traditional Hadoop MapReduce, leading to substantial performance gains for many types of workloads.

Spark's architecture revolves around a distributed data abstraction that has evolved over time.

Resilient Distributed Datasets (RDDs): The foundational data structure in Spark, RDDs are immutable, fault-tolerant collections of data that are partitioned across the cluster. They provide a low-level API for distributed data manipulation.

DataFrames and Datasets: Building upon RDDs, DataFrames and Datasets offer higher-level, structured APIs for working with data. DataFrames provide a tabular data structure with schema inference, while Datasets offer type safety and object-oriented programming capabilities. These higher-level abstractions enable more efficient data manipulation and optimization through Spark's Catalyst query optimizer.

Spark excels at large-scale batch processing, efficiently handling massive datasets stored in various sources like HDFS, object stores (e.g., S3), and traditional databases. Its ability to distribute computations across a large cluster and its optimized execution engine make it well-suited for tasks like ETL (Extract, Transform, Load), data warehousing, and large-scale data transformations.

Furthermore, Spark provides robust support for fault tolerance through its lineage tracking mechanism. If a partition of data is lost due to a node failure, Spark can reconstruct that partition by replaying the sequence of transformations (the lineage) that led to it. This inherent fault tolerance ensures the reliability and resilience of Spark-based data pipelines.

Spark's rich ecosystem of libraries further enhances its versatility:

MLlib: A comprehensive machine learning library providing a wide range of algorithms for classification, regression, clustering, collaborative filtering, and more.

GraphX: A library for graph processing and analysis, enabling tasks like social network analysis, recommendation systems, and pathfinding algorithms.

Spark SQL: A module for working with structured data using SQL queries, providing integration with various data sources and enabling efficient data querying and analysis.

Structured Streaming: A powerful extension for building scalable and fault-tolerant stream processing applications using the same DataFrame/Dataset API as batch processing. It utilizes a micro-batching approach, processing streams in small, discrete intervals.

Spark's ability to seamlessly integrate with various data sources and its extensive library ecosystem make it a highly adaptable and popular choice for a wide range of petabyte-scale workloads, from complex data science workflows to large-scale data engineering pipelines.

Apache Flink: The Stateful Stream Processing Powerhouse

Apache Flink distinguishes itself as a stateful stream processing engine meticulously designed for high-throughput and true low-latency processing of continuous data streams. Unlike Spark's micro-batching approach to streaming, Flink processes individual events as they arrive, offering significantly lower end-to-end latency, often measured in milliseconds. This makes it ideal for real-time applications where immediate insights and actions are critical.

A key strength of Flink lies in its strong guarantees for exactly once processing. This ensures that each event in the data stream is processed exactly once, even in the face of system failures. This is crucial for applications where data integrity and accuracy are paramount, such as financial transaction processing or real-time fraud detection.

Flink's sophisticated state management capabilities are another defining characteristic. Many complex event processing and real-time analytics tasks require maintaining and updating state over time. Flink provides robust mechanisms for managing application state in a fault-tolerant and scalable manner, allowing for complex windowing, aggregations, and pattern matching on continuous data streams.

While initially focused on stream processing, Flink also offers robust batch processing capabilities through its unified dataflow model. This means that both streaming and batch computations are treated as special cases of the same underlying dataflow paradigm. This unified approach allows organizations to leverage a single engine for both real-time and historical analytics, simplifying their infrastructure and development efforts.

Flink's architecture is built around a distributed runtime that efficiently executes dataflow graphs. It employs techniques like pipelining and operator chaining to minimize latency and maximize throughput. Its focus on true stream processing and state management makes it a compelling choice for organizations seeking to build highly responsive and accurate real-time applications on a scale, such as:

Real-time analytics dashboards: Providing up-to-the-second insights into key business metrics.

Complex event processing (CEP): Identifying patterns and correlations in real-time event streams.

Real-time fraud detection: Analyzing transactions as they occur to identify and prevent fraudulent activity.

Stream-based machine learning: Training and deploying machine learning models on continuous data streams.

Dask: Native Python Parallelism for Scalable Data Science

Dask takes a different approach compared to Spark and Flink. Rather than being a standalone processing engine with its own runtime and programming model, Dask is a flexible parallel computing library for Python that scales natively within the Python ecosystem. Its core philosophy is to parallelize existing Python data science workflows with minimal code changes.

Dask can leverage familiar Python libraries like NumPy, Pandas, and Scikit-learn to parallelize computations across multi-core CPUs on a single machine or across distributed clusters of machines. This tight integration with the Python ecosystem makes it particularly attractive to data scientists and analysts who are already comfortable working with these libraries and want to scale their existing workflows to handle datasets that are too large to fit into memory.

Dask excels at interactive data exploration and analysis on out-of-core datasets. Its lazy evaluation mechanism means that computations are only performed when the results are explicitly needed. This allows users to work with datasets larger than RAM without encountering memory errors. Dask's task scheduling system efficiently manages the parallel execution of computations across available resources.

Key features of Dask include:

Dask DataFrames: Parallelized Pandas DataFrames that can operate on datasets larger than memory.

Dask Arrays: Parallelized NumPy arrays for large numerical computations.

Dask ML: Parallelized machine learning algorithms that integrate with Scikit-learn.

Dask Delayed: A low-level API for parallelizing arbitrary Python functions.

Dask's strength lies in its ease of use for Python developers and its ability to seamlessly scale existing Python-based data science workflows. It is particularly well-suited for:

Interactive data analysis on large datasets: Allowing data scientists to explore and manipulate data that doesn't fit in memory.

Parallelizing computationally intensive Python tasks: Accelerating machine learning model training and other data processing pipelines.

Prototyping and iterating on scalable data science solutions: Providing a familiar environment for developing and testing scalable algorithms.

Apache Spark, Apache Flink, and Dask represent distinct yet powerful approaches to petabyte-scale data processing. Spark offers a versatile and mature platform for a wide range of workloads, excelling in batch processing and providing strong capabilities for stream processing and machine learning. Flink stands out with its focus on true low-latency, stateful stream processing, making it ideal for real-time applications demanding high throughput and exactly-once guarantees. Dask provides a seamless way for Python users to scale their existing data science workflows to handle large datasets and parallel computations within the familiar Python ecosystem. The choice of which engine to adopt depends heavily on the specific requirements of the workload, the desired latency, the existing infrastructure, and the expertise of the development team. Often, organizations may even leverage a combination of these engines to address the diverse needs of their petabyte-scale data analytics initiatives.

Serverless Data Processing: Event-Driven Workflows at Scale

Serverless compute options, exemplified by AWS Lambda, represent a significant departure from traditional, long-running server-based data processing infrastructure, offering a compelling paradigm particularly well-suited for event-driven workflows at scale. These services empower developers to execute code in direct response to specific events, such as the arrival of new data in object storage (like S3), the appearance of a message in a message queue (like SQS or Kafka), changes in a database (via database triggers), or even scheduled events. The defining characteristic of serverless is the complete abstraction of the underlying infrastructure: developers focus solely on writing and deploying their code, while the cloud provider transparently handles all aspects of server provisioning, scaling, patching, and maintenance.

This fundamental shift offers several key advantages for data processing, especially in the context of petabyte-scale data:

Automatic and Elastic Scalability: One of the most significant benefits of serverless data processing is its inherent ability to automatically scale in response to the volume of incoming events. As the rate of data arrival or the number of messages in a queue increases, the serverless platform dynamically allocates more computing resources to handle the increased load. Conversely, when there are no events to process, the compute resources scale down to zero, leading to significant cost optimization. This elasticity is crucial for handling the often unpredictable and bursty nature of data streams and event-driven pipelines at petabyte scale, where manual scaling adjustments can be cumbersome and reactive.

Cost Efficiency: The pricing model of serverless compute is typically based on actual execution time and the number of invocations. You only pay for the compute resources consumed while your code is running, down to the millisecond in some cases. This "pay-as-you-go" model can be significantly more cost-effective than maintaining always-on server instances, especially for workloads with intermittent activity or variable loads. For petabyte-scale data processing, where vast amounts of data might trigger numerous processing tasks, the granular billing of serverless can lead to substantial cost savings compared to continuously running large clusters.

By abstracting away the underlying infrastructure, serverless drastically reduces operational complexity and overhead. Developers and data engineers are freed from the burdens of server provisioning, configuration, patching, monitoring, and capacity planning. This allows them to focus their efforts on building and optimizing their data processing logic, leading to faster development cycles and reduced management overhead. For petabyte-scale deployments, managing the infrastructure for traditional processing engines can be a significant undertaking; serverless alleviates much of this burden.

Event-Driven Architecture: Serverless functions are inherently event-driven, making them a natural fit for building reactive data processing pipelines. They can be easily triggered by a wide range of events from various data sources and services within the cloud ecosystem. This allows for the creation of loosely coupled and highly responsive architectures where data flows trigger specific processing tasks in a modular and scalable manner. For petabyte-scale data, this event-driven approach can be used to orchestrate complex workflows where different stages of processing are triggered by the completion of previous stages or the arrival of specific data subsets.

Building Complex Pipelines Through Chaining: While individual serverless function executions are typically designed to be short-lived (often with configurable time limits), complex data processing pipelines can be constructed by chaining together multiple serverless functions. The output of one function can trigger the invocation of another, allowing for the sequential or parallel execution of different data transformation or enrichment steps. Services like AWS Step Functions provide orchestration capabilities to manage these complex workflows, defining state machines and handling error conditions. For petabyte-scale processing, this modularity allows for breaking down large, complex tasks into smaller, manageable, and independently scalable serverless units.

Integration with Scalable Storage and Processing Services: Serverless options rarely operate in isolation for petabyte-scale workloads. They often work in conjunction with other highly scalable storage and processing services. For example:

Data Ingestion: Serverless functions can be triggered by the arrival of new data in object storage (like S3) or data streams (like Kinesis) to perform initial data validation, transformation, or routing.

Real-time Data Enrichment: As data streams through services like Kinesis, serverless functions can be invoked for each record to perform real-time lookups, enrich the data with additional context from databases or external APIs, and then forward the enriched data to downstream processing or storage.

Triggering Downstream Processing: The completion of a batch processing job on a large dataset (e.g., in Spark or EMR) can trigger a serverless function to perform post-processing steps, update metadata, or initiate downstream analytics.

Microservices for Data Processing: Serverless functions can be used to build fine-grained data processing microservices, each responsible for a specific transformation or task, which can be orchestrated to handle petabyte-scale data flows.

Limitations and Considerations for Petabyte Scale:

While serverless offers significant advantages, there are also limitations and considerations to keep in mind for petabyte-scale data processing:

Execution Time Limits: Most serverless platforms impose limits on the maximum execution duration of a single function invocation. For very long-running data transformations, this might necessitate breaking down the work into smaller, chained functions.

Memory and Compute Limits: Individual serverless functions also have limitations on the amount of memory and compute resources they can consume. Processing extremely large individual records or performing highly intensive computations within a single function might not be feasible.

Cold Starts: The first invocation of a serverless function after a period of inactivity can experience a "cold start," where there is a slight delay as the underlying environment is initialized. While this is often in the order of milliseconds or seconds, it can be a concern for latency-sensitive real-time processing.

State Management: Serverless functions are typically designed to be stateless. Managing state across multiple invocations or within a complex pipeline requires the use of external state management services.

Complexity of Orchestration: For intricate petabyte-scale data pipelines involving numerous serverless functions, managing the orchestration and dependencies can become complex, requiring robust workflow management tools.

Data Locality: Moving large volumes of data to and from serverless functions for processing can introduce latency and incur data transfer costs. Optimizing data locality is crucial for performance.

Serverless data processing offers a powerful and flexible paradigm for building event-driven workflows at scale, particularly when integrated with other scalable storage and processing services. Its automatic scalability, cost efficiency, reduced operational overhead, and inherent event-driven nature make it an attractive option for various aspects of petabyte-scale data pipelines, such as real-time data enrichment, triggering downstream processes, and building microservices for data transformation. While considerations around execution limits, state management, and orchestration are important, serverless compute provides a valuable tool in the arsenal of organizations seeking to efficiently and cost-effectively process the ever-growing volumes of data in the petabyte era.

Optimization Techniques for Efficient Petabyte-Scale Processing

Achieving efficient petabyte-scale processing requires not only choosing the right framework but also employing various optimization techniques:

Partitioning: Data partitioning involves dividing large datasets into smaller, more manageable chunks based on certain criteria, such as time, geographical location, or a specific key. This allows processing frameworks to distribute the workload across multiple nodes more effectively, as each node can operate on a subset of the data in parallel. Proper partitioning strategies can significantly improve query performance and reduce the amount of data that needs to be scanned or processed for a given task.

Indexing: Indexing is a technique used to speed up data retrieval by creating data structures that allow for faster lookups based on specific columns or attributes. While traditionally associated with databases, indexing techniques can also be applied to large-scale data processing frameworks. For example, creating indexes on frequently queried columns in a data lake can significantly accelerate analytical queries. Choosing the right columns to index and the type of index to use depends on the specific query patterns and data access requirements.

Vectorized Execution: Vectorized execution is a performance optimization technique that processes data in batches or vectors rather than one row at a time. This can significantly reduce the overhead of function calls and improve the efficiency of data processing operations. Modern data processing engines like Spark and vectorized query engines in data warehouses leverage vectorized execution to accelerate analytical queries on large datasets.

Processing petabytes of data efficiently and with minimal latency is a cornerstone of extracting meaningful insights from massive datasets. Modern data processing frameworks like Apache Spark, Flink, and Dask provide powerful tools for achieving parallelism and scalability. The emergence of serverless compute options offers a flexible and event-driven approach for specific data processing tasks. However, the choice of framework is only the first step. Optimizing data processing pipelines through strategic partitioning, intelligent indexing, and leveraging techniques like vectorized execution are crucial for maximizing performance and minimizing resource consumption at petabyte scale. As organizations continue to generate and analyze ever-increasing volumes of data, the ability to orchestrate efficient data transformation through these powerful frameworks and optimization techniques will be a key differentiator in their ability to derive value and maintain a competitive edge in the data-driven era.

CHAPTER SEVEN

ORCHESTRATING COMPLEX DATA WORKFLOWS

T his chapter delves into the realm of workflow orchestration tools, examining prominent platforms such as Apache Airflow, Prefect, and Dagster. We will dissect best practices for achieving comprehensive pipeline observability, implementing effective retry mechanisms to ensure resilience, and strategies for managing long-running jobs without introducing performance bottlenecks, ultimately aiming to provide a blueprint for building robust and manageable data workflows on an extreme scale.

At petabyte scale, data workflows often involve a multitude of interconnected tasks, spanning data ingestion from diverse sources, complex transformations and aggregations across vast datasets, machine learning model training and deployment, and the serving of processed data to various downstream applications and analytical dashboards. These pipelines can be characterized by intricate dependencies, where the successful completion of one task is a prerequisite for the initiation of subsequent steps. The sheer volume of data being processed necessitates distributed execution across numerous compute resources, introducing complexities in managing task dependencies across these distributed environments.

Furthermore, the need for timely and reliable data delivery often imposes strict scheduling requirements. Pipelines may need to run at specific intervals (hourly, daily, weekly), triggered by external events, or dependent on the completion of upstream data availability. Managing these schedules across a large number of pipelines, each with its own unique timing and dependency constraints, requires sophisticated orchestration capabilities.

The inherent complexity and distributed nature of petabyte-scale pipelines make monitoring and debugging a significant challenge. Identifying the root cause of failures, tracking the progress of long-running jobs, and gaining visibility into the overall health and performance of the workflow require robust monitoring and observability tools. Without effective orchestration, these complex data workflows can easily become unmanageable, prone to failures, and difficult to troubleshoot, hindering the agility and reliability of the entire data platform.

Workflow Orchestration Tools: Guiding the Flow of Data

The sheer volume and velocity of data at this scale necessitate robust and scalable orchestration solutions that can handle the complexity of multi-stage processing, diverse technology integrations, and the inherent challenges of distributed computing.

Apache Airflow's enduring popularity stems not only from its open-source nature and extensive community but also from its well-defined architecture and its ability to represent intricate dependencies through DAGs. The Python-based DSL, while offering immense flexibility, also requires a degree of programming proficiency, and managing very large and complex DAGs can sometimes lead to maintenance overhead and challenges in visualization. Airflow's scheduler, while robust, relies on a centralized approach, which can become a bottleneck at extreme scale if not properly configured and managed. However, the vast ecosystem of operators and sensors significantly simplifies integration with a multitude of data sources, processing engines like Spark and Flink, data warehouses, and cloud-specific services. This broad connectivity is paramount in petabyte-scale environments where data often resides in disparate systems and requires processing through a variety of specialized tools. The maturity of Airflow also means a wealth of community-contributed resources, best practices, and battle-tested solutions for common challenges encountered at scale. Features like task retries, branching, and sub-DAGs allow for the creation of resilient and sophisticated workflows capable of handling failures and conditional execution paths, crucial for the reliability of petabyte-scale pipelines.

Prefect's modern design philosophy addresses some of the perceived limitations of earlier orchestration tools by emphasizing dynamic workflow creation and a more intuitive Python-centric approach. The use of decorators to define tasks and flows allows developers to leverage their existing Python knowledge more directly. Prefect's dynamic task mapping is particularly advantageous when dealing with petabyte-scale datasets that might be partitioned or processed in a variable number of parallel tasks. The centralized cloud offering provides a streamlined experience for monitoring and managing workflows, abstracting away some of the infrastructure management complexities. Prefect's focus on observability, with rich logging and visualization, is essential for understanding the execution of complex pipelines and pinpointing potential issues on a scale. The built-in support for features like automatic retries with exponential backoff, sophisticated error handling, and parameterized workflows contributes to the robustness and adaptability required for managing petabyte-scale data processing where failures can be costly and re-processing large volumes of data can be time-consuming.

Dagster's unique emphasis on data lineage and software-defined assets brings a different perspective to workflow orchestration, particularly relevant in data-intensive environments. By explicitly defining the inputs and outputs of each "solid" and tracking the lineage of data transformations, Dagster provides a clearer understanding of the data's journey through the pipeline. This lineage information is invaluable for debugging issues, ensuring data quality, and meeting compliance requirements in petabyte-scale scenarios where data governance is critical. The focus on type safety and testability promotes the development of more reliable and maintainable data pipelines, reducing the risk of errors when dealing with massive datasets. Dagster's built-in UI offers detailed insights into asset materialization, providing a higher-level view of the data's lifecycle and the success of its processing. The support for incremental processing can significantly optimize the execution of petabyte-scale pipelines by avoiding the need to re-process unchanged data. Dagster's strong emphasis on modularity and composability encourages the creation of well-structured and reusable data processing components, simplifying the management of complex workflows at scale.

In conclusion, the selection of a workflow orchestration tool for petabyte-scale data pipelines is a strategic decision with significant implications for efficiency, reliability, and maintainability. While Apache Airflow offers a mature and widely adopted platform with extensive integrations, Prefect provides a modern, Python-centric approach with a focus on dynamic workflows and observability. Dagster distinguishes itself with its emphasis on data lineage, type safety, and software-defined assets. The optimal choice often depends on the specific needs and priorities of the organization, including the existing technology stack, the complexity and dynamism of the data pipelines, the importance of data governance and lineage, and the team's development preferences. In many cases, organizations might even find themselves leveraging a combination of these tools to address the diverse orchestration requirements of their petabyte-scale data processing landscape.

Best Practices for Robust Workflow Orchestration

Pipeline Observability, at the petabyte scale, transcends basic logging and monitoring. It necessitates a proactive and holistic approach to understanding the intricate dance of data as it moves through the pipeline. Comprehensive logging should include not only technical details but also business-relevant context, enabling stakeholders to understand the impact of processing steps. Advanced metrics should track not just resource utilization but also data quality metrics at each stage, providing early warnings of potential data integrity issues. Real-time visualizations should offer dynamic insights into data flow and processing bottlenecks, allowing for immediate intervention. Furthermore, incorporating alerting mechanisms based on predefined thresholds for performance degradation or error rates is crucial for proactive issue detection and resolution, minimizing downtime, and ensuring the timely delivery of processed data. Effective observability at this scale requires a well-integrated suite of tools and a dedicated team capable of interpreting the vast amounts of information generated.

Retry mechanisms, while seemingly straightforward, demand careful consideration in petabyte-scale environments. Aggressive retry strategies without proper backoff and jitter can exacerbate the load on already struggling services, potentially leading to cascading failures. The configuration of retry policies should be intelligent, taking into account the nature of the failure (transient network issue vs. fundamental processing error) and the criticality of the task. Implementing circuit breaker patterns can prevent repeated attempts to access a consistently failing service, providing it with time to recover. Moreover, logging failed attempts with sufficient context is essential for post-mortem analysis and identifying systemic issues that require more than just retries to resolve. At this scale, the orchestration framework should also provide mechanisms for manual intervention and debugging of persistently failing tasks.

Handling long-running jobs at petabyte scale necessitates sophisticated checkpointing strategies. Checkpoints should be frequent enough to minimize data re-processing in case of failure but not so frequent as to introduce significant overhead. The orchestration tool should manage the storage and retrieval of these checkpoints efficiently. Furthermore, the ability to dynamically scale the resources allocated to long-running tasks based on their progress and remaining workload can optimize resource utilization and reduce overall processing time. Breaking down monolithic jobs into finer-grained, parallelizable units not only improves resilience but also allows for more efficient resource allocation and faster overall completion times. The orchestration framework should provide abstractions that simplify the management and coordination of these parallel tasks.

Dependency management in petabyte-scale pipelines becomes exponentially more complex with the increasing number of tasks and interconnected workflows. The orchestration tool must provide clear and intuitive ways to define and visualize these dependencies, even across different sub-pipelines. Robust mechanisms for enforcing these dependencies are crucial to prevent out-of-order execution and ensure data consistency. Features like conditional branching and parallel execution based on data characteristics or external triggers add further complexity but are often necessary to optimize processing for diverse datasets. Effective dependency management at this scale requires a well-defined workflow design and potentially the use of sub-workflows or modular DAGs to improve maintainability and understandability.

Idempotency in individual tasks is not just a best practice but a fundamental requirement for reliably processing petabytes of data. Without it, retries and partial failures can lead to significant data duplication, inconsistencies, and ultimately, unreliable analytical results. Achieving idempotency often requires careful design of the underlying data processing logic, potentially involving tracking processed records or using atomic operations. The orchestration framework can assist by providing mechanisms for tracking task execution and ensuring that retried tasks can safely resume or re-execute without adverse effects. Thorough testing of the idempotency of critical tasks is essential at this scale.

Resource management at the petabyte scale directly impacts both performance and cost. Inefficient resource allocation can lead to prolonged processing times and exorbitant cloud bills. Orchestration tools should provide granular control over resource requests for individual tasks, allowing for optimization based on the specific computational needs of each step. Integration with the auto-scaling capabilities of underlying compute platforms is crucial for dynamically adjusting resources based on workload fluctuations. Cost awareness should be built into the orchestration framework, providing insights into resource consumption and potential cost optimizations.

Treating Workflow Definitions as Code with robust version control and CI/CD practices becomes even more critical at petabyte scale due to the increased complexity and the potential impact of errors. Automated testing of workflow definitions should include not only syntax and logic checks but also integration tests with representative datasets. CI/CD pipelines should automate the deployment of validated workflow updates across different environments, ensuring consistency and reducing the risk of manual errors. Rollback mechanisms are also essential for quickly reverting to stable versions in case of issues with new deployments. Effective version control and CI/CD for workflows enable agility and reduce the risk associated with managing and updating complex petabyte-scale data pipelines.

Orchestrating petabyte-scale data pipelines demands a comprehensive and rigorous application of these best practices. The scale amplifies the importance of observability, resilience, correctness, efficiency, and maintainability. A well-chosen orchestration tool, coupled with a deep understanding and consistent application of these principles, is essential for transforming vast amounts of raw data into valuable insights in a reliable and cost-effective manner.

Mastering the Flow of Petabyte-Scale Data

Orchestrating complex data workflows at petabyte scale transcends mere automation; it embodies a critical discipline that transforms raw, distributed processing capabilities into reliable, efficient, and ultimately, valuable data pipelines. Without robust orchestration, the potential of powerful processing engines and scalable storage solutions remains largely untapped, akin to having a high-performance engine without a skilled driver and a clear roadmap. Workflow orchestration tools, with prominent examples like Apache Airflow, Prefect, and Dagster, provide the essential frameworks for programmatically defining, meticulously scheduling, and comprehensively monitoring these intricate data processing sequences. They act as the conductor of a data symphony, ensuring that each instrument (task) plays its part at the right time and in harmony with the others.

The significance of effective orchestration becomes exponentially pronounced at the petabyte scale. The sheer volume and velocity of data, coupled with the distributed nature of the underlying infrastructure, introduce a multitude of potential points of failure and complexities. Without a well-defined orchestration strategy, data pipelines can become brittle, prone to errors, difficult to debug, and incredibly challenging to manage and scale. This can lead to delays in data delivery, inconsistencies in analytical results, increased operational costs, and ultimately, a failure to extract timely and meaningful insights from the organization's most valuable asset its data.

Adhering to best practices in pipeline observability forms the cornerstone of reliable petabyte-scale workflows. The ability to gain deep and granular insights into the execution of every task, the flow of data, and the health of the underlying infrastructure is paramount. Comprehensive logging, capturing not just system-level information but also business-relevant context, provides an auditable trail and aids in understanding the lineage of data transformations. Detailed metrics, tracking resource utilization, processing times, data volumes, and even data quality indicators at each stage, enable proactive performance monitoring and the early detection of anomalies or bottlenecks. Clear and intuitive visualizations of pipeline progress, task status, and historical trends provide an at-a-glance understanding of the workflow's overall health and facilitate quicker diagnosis of issues. Robust observability empowers data engineers and operators to anticipate problems, debug failures efficiently, and optimize pipeline performance for maximum throughput and cost-effectiveness.

Implementing robust retry mechanisms is not merely a safeguard but a fundamental requirement for building resilient petabyte-scale data pipelines. The inherent transient nature of distributed systems means that occasional failures are inevitable. Orchestration frameworks must be configured to automatically handle these transient errors by retrying failed tasks with intelligent backoff strategies, preventing cascading failures, and ensuring that pipelines can recover gracefully. The configuration of retry policies should be nuanced, considering the type of failure and the criticality of the task. Well-designed retry mechanisms, coupled with effective logging of retry attempts, contribute significantly to the overall stability and reliability of data workflows at scale, minimizing the need for manual intervention and ensuring timely data processing.

Effectively managing long-running jobs is a unique challenge in petabyte-scale processing. Tasks that involve processing massive datasets or performing complex computations can take extended periods to complete, increasing their susceptibility to interruptions. Orchestration tools must provide sophisticated mechanisms for checkpointing the progress of these long-running jobs, allowing them to resume from the last successful state in the event of failures. This prevents the wasteful re-processing of vast amounts of data and significantly improves the efficiency and resilience of the pipeline. Furthermore, the ability to break down these monolithic tasks into smaller, parallelizable units, coordinated by the orchestration framework, can dramatically reduce overall processing time and enhance manageability.

Carefully defining task dependencies is the architectural blueprint of a well-orchestrated data pipeline. Orchestration tools utilize DAGs or similar constructs to explicitly represent the order in which tasks must execute and the relationships between them. Ensuring that tasks only begin execution after their upstream dependencies have been successfully completed is crucial for maintaining data consistency and the logical integrity of the workflow. Clear and accurate dependency management prevents data corruption, ensures that downstream tasks operate on correctly transformed data, and simplifies the understanding and maintenance of complex pipelines.

By adhering to these best practices and leveraging the capabilities of modern workflow orchestration tools, organizations can transform their raw data processing capabilities into reliable and valuable data pipelines capable of handling the immense scale and complexity of petabyte-scale data. Mastering the flow of this data through well-orchestrated pipelines is not just a technical necessity; it is a strategic imperative for unlocking the full potential of data-driven insights, fostering innovation, achieving agility in the face of evolving business demands, and ultimately gaining a competitive advantage in the data-rich landscape of the modern era. The ability to effectively orchestrate petabyte-scale data workflows is a key differentiator for organizations seeking to thrive in the age of big data.

CHAPTER EIGHT

REAL-TIME AND BATCH PROCESSING TRADE-OFFS

In the realm of petabyte-scale data platforms, the decision of how and when to process data in the immediate, continuous flow of real-time or in the deliberate, bulk operations of batch processing represents a fundamental architectural trade-off with profound implications for system design, performance, cost, and the timeliness of derived insights. While the allure of real-time processing for immediate action and up-to-the-second analytics is increasingly compelling, but batch processing remains an indispensable workhorse for large-scale historical analysis and computationally intensive transformations. This chapter delves into the inherent trade-offs between these two processing paradigms, explores the hybrid architectural patterns notably the Lambda and Kappa architectures, that seek to leverage the strengths of both, and provides guidance on when to strategically employ each approach. Furthermore, we will examine critical techniques for incremental processing to optimize batch workloads and the challenges and strategies for maintaining data consistency across systems employing both real-time and batch processing methodologies.

The Dichotomy of Time: Understanding Real Time and Batch Processing

The dichotomy of time, as it relates to data processing, fundamentally distinguishes between real-time and batch processing, representing two contrasting yet often complementary approaches to extracting value from data. These paradigms differ significantly in their temporal characteristics, processing methodologies, and suitability for various application domains. Understanding this dichotomy is crucial for designing effective data architectures that can address a wide range of analytical and operational needs.

At its core, batch processing operates on the principle of accumulating data over a specific, often predefined period. This collection window can range from minutes to hours, days, or even longer, depending on the specific use case and the rate at which data is generated. Once this defined period concludes, the entire accumulated dataset is treated as a discrete unit and subjected to bulk processing. This typically involves reading the data from its storage location, performing a series of transformations, aggregations, and analyses, and then writing the results to another storage system or generating reports.

One of the primary characteristics of batch processing is its inherent ability to handle massive volumes of data efficiently. By processing data in bulk, systems can optimize resource utilization, leveraging distributed processing frameworks like Apache Spark or traditional MapReduce to parallelize computations across numerous nodes. This parallel processing capability allows for complex transformations and aggregations to be performed on petabyte-scale datasets within reasonable timeframes. Batch processing is particularly well-suited for tasks that require analyzing large historical datasets, such as generating daily or weekly reports, performing end-of-month financial reconciliations, building and training machine learning models on historical data, and populating data warehouses for business intelligence.

However, the fundamental trade-off in batch processing is the inherent latency introduced by the data collection window. The insights derived from batch processing are, by definition, delayed, reflecting a historical snapshot of the data up to the point when the processing batch commenced. This latency can range from minutes to days, rendering batch processing unsuitable for applications that require immediate responses to incoming data. The insights gained are valuable for trend analysis, strategic decision-making, and understanding past performance, but they lack the immediacy required for real-time interventions or dynamic adjustments.

Real-Time Processing: The Urgency of Immediate Insights

In stark contrast to batch processing, real-time processing focuses on the continuous processing of individual data events as they arrive. The primary goal is to generate immediate insights and enable near-instantaneous actions based on the most up-to-date information. This paradigm is essential for a growing number of modern applications that demand immediate responsiveness to continuous data streams. Examples include fraud detection systems that need to identify and flag suspicious transactions as they occur, anomaly detection systems that need to identify unusual patterns in real-time sensor data, personalized recommendation engines that need to adapt suggestions based on immediate user behavior, and real-time monitoring dashboards that need to display up-to-the-second metrics.

Real-time systems typically require low-latency data ingestion and processing pipelines. This often involves the use of stream processing engines like Apache Flink, Apache Kafka Streams, or specialized cloud services that are designed to handle high data velocity and process individual events with minimal delay. These engines often employ techniques like in-memory processing and pipelined execution to achieve the required low latency. Furthermore, many real-time applications require maintaining state to perform complex event correlation, such as identifying patterns of events occurring within a specific time window or tracking user sessions.

However, achieving consistency, handling out-of-order events (where data arrives in a sequence different from when it was generated), and managing the complexities of distributed state in real-time systems can be significantly more challenging than in batch processing. Ensuring data integrity and accurate state updates across a distributed stream processing cluster in the face of failures requires sophisticated techniques like checkpointing and state replication. Dealing with out-of-order events often necessitates the implementation of windowing and buffering mechanisms to ensure that events are processed in the correct temporal context. The continuous nature of real-time processing also demands robust fault tolerance and scalability to handle fluctuating data volumes and ensure uninterrupted operation.

The Blurring Lines and Complementary Nature

It's important to note that the lines between real-time and batch processing are not always absolute and are increasingly blurring. Hybrid architectures are becoming common, where batch processing is used for historical analysis and model building, while real-time processing is employed for immediate decision-making and operational responsiveness. For instance, a recommendation engine might use batch processing to train its models on historical user behavior and then use real-time processing to adapt recommendations based on a user's current interactions.

Furthermore, some modern data processing frameworks are attempting to unify batch and stream processing within a single engine, offering the flexibility to handle both historical and real-time data with varying latency requirements. Understanding the strengths and weaknesses of each approach and how they can be effectively combined is crucial for building robust and versatile data processing systems that can meet the diverse needs of modern data-driven organizations. The choice between real-time and batch processing, or a combination thereof, ultimately depends on the specific application requirements, the nature of the data, and the desired timeliness of the insights.

Bridging the Divide: Hybrid Architectures for Optimal Data Utilization

Bridging the divide between the temporal extremes of real-time and batch processing has led to the emergence of hybrid architectures, pragmatic solutions that aim to harness the complementary strengths of both approaches to achieve optimal data utilization. Recognizing that neither real-time nor batch processing alone can satisfy all analytical and operational requirements, these hybrid models strive to provide a comprehensive data platform capable of delivering both historical insights and immediate responsiveness. Two prominent examples of such hybrid architectures are the Lambda Architecture and the Kappa Architecture.

The Lambda Architecture, conceived to address the limitations of purely batch-oriented systems in handling real-time data needs, proposes maintaining two parallel and distinct processing pipelines for all incoming data: a batch processing path and a speed (or real-time) processing path.

The batch layer is responsible for processing the entire historical dataset. It operates on a scheduled basis, typically performing complex transformations and aggregations on the accumulated data to generate accurate and comprehensive views. This layer prioritizes accuracy and the ability to process massive volumes of data, often leveraging distributed processing frameworks like Hadoop or Spark. The output of the batch layer is typically stored in a serving layer optimized for querying historical data.

The speed layer, on the other hand, focuses on processing only the most recent, incoming data streams. Its primary goal is to provide low-latency updates and enable near real-time insights. This layer often employs stream processing engines like Apache Storm, Flink, or Spark Streaming to process events as they arrive. The speed layer compensates for the inherent latency of the batch layer by providing a near real-time view of the data, albeit potentially with less comprehensive transformations or aggregations compared to the batch layer. The output of the speed layer is also made available in the serving layer.

The serving layer sits atop both the batch and speed layers. Its responsibility is to merge the results from these two parallel pipelines to provide a unified view of both historical and near real-time data to the end user or application. This merging can happen at query time or through pre-computation. The Lambda architecture effectively addresses the latency limitations of batch processing for real-time use cases by providing a separate, low-latency path while still leveraging the power of batch processing for comprehensive historical analysis and accuracy.

However, the Lambda architecture introduces significant complexity. Maintaining two separate codebases, one for the batch layer and another for the speed layer, can be challenging. Ensuring consistency in the processing logic and the resulting data between these two layers is a critical concern and requires careful design and implementation. Debugging and operating two distinct pipelines also add to the operational overhead.

The Kappa Architecture: A Unified Streaming Vision

The Kappa Architecture emerged as a simplification of the Lambda Architecture, advocating for a single, unified stream processing pipeline to handle all data, both historical and real-time. In this model, the fundamental principle is that all data, regardless of its age or arrival time, is treated as an immutable stream of events.

Instead of maintaining a separate batch layer, historical analysis in the Kappa Architecture is performed by replaying the entire historical data stream through the same stream processing engine used for real-time data. This requires the ability to store the entire raw data stream in a durable and scalable manner, often utilizing distributed log systems like Apache Kafka as the central data hub.

The stream processing engine in the Kappa Architecture is responsible for consuming this unified data stream, performing the necessary transformations and aggregations, and making the results available for querying. To perform historical analysis or to recalculate results due to changes in processing logic or bug fixes, the entire historical stream is simply reprocessed.

The Kappa Architecture offers the significant advantage of eliminating the need to maintain two separate codebases, thus simplifying development and reducing operational complexity compared to the Lambda Architecture. The single pipeline approach can also lead to more consistent data processing and a more streamlined architecture.

However, the Kappa Architecture places a significant burden on the stream processing engine. It must be capable of handling both the continuous low-latency processing of real-time data and the potentially massive task of reprocessing the entire historical dataset. This requires a stream processing engine with high throughput, scalability, and the ability to manage large amounts of state. Furthermore, the time required to reprocess the entire historical stream for analysis or reprocessing can be substantial, potentially introducing latency for certain types of historical queries, although the real-time data remains immediately available.

Bridging the Divide: Choosing the Right Hybrid Approach

Both the Lambda and Kappa architectures represent valuable approaches to bridging the divide between real-time and batch processing, each with its own set of trade-offs. The choice between them often depends on the specific requirements of the data platform, the nature of the use cases, the capabilities of the available technologies, and the development and operational resources.

Organizations that have existing batch processing infrastructure and are looking to add real-time capabilities might find the Lambda Architecture a more natural evolution, despite its complexity. On the other hand, organizations building data platforms from scratch or those with a strong emphasis on stream processing might lean towards the simplicity and unified nature of the Kappa Architecture, provided their stream processing engine can handle the demands of reprocessing historical data.

Ultimately, the goal of these hybrid architectures is to achieve optimal data utilization by providing a comprehensive platform that can deliver both the immediacy of real-time insights and the depth and accuracy of historical analysis, catering to a wider range of business needs and analytical requirements. The ongoing evolution of data processing technologies continues to blur the lines and offer new hybrid patterns that aim to further simplify and optimize the handling of both streaming and batch data at scale.

Strategic Selection: When to Employ Real-Time vs. Batch Processing

The strategic selection between real-time, batch, or a hybrid data processing approach is fundamentally driven by the specific demands and characteristics of the intended use case. Each paradigm offers distinct advantages and limitations that make it more or less suitable for different scenarios.

Real-time processing emerges as the ideal choice when the temporal aspect of data is paramount. Situations demanding immediate action, such as the critical need to identify and respond to fraudulent transactions or security intrusions as they occur, necessitate the low latency inherent in real-time analysis. Similarly, applications where up-to-the-second insights are critical, like real-time dashboards providing live operational metrics or monitoring systems tracking critical infrastructure, rely on the continuous processing of incoming data streams. Furthermore, personalization that needs immediate context, such as dynamically adjusting product recommendations based on a user's current browsing behavior or tailoring content based on their immediate interactions, benefits significantly from the instantaneous analysis of real-time events. Finally, applications with strict latency requirements, such as high-frequency trading platforms or real-time bidding systems in advertising, cannot tolerate the delays associated with batch processing and demand near-instantaneous processing of individual data points.

Conversely, batch processing remains a critical workhorse for a distinct set of use cases where the focus shifts from immediacy to scale and comprehensive analysis. Large-scale historical analysis, such as identifying long-term business trends spanning years of data, performing in-depth cohort analysis to understand user behavior over time, or generating comprehensive financial or operational reports, often necessitates the processing of massive datasets in bulk. Complex transformations and aggregations, particularly computationally intensive tasks like Extract, Transform, Load (ETL) processes for populating data warehouses or training sophisticated machine learning models on vast historical datasets, are typically more efficiently handled through batch processing's ability to leverage distributed computing frameworks. Moreover, ensuring data accuracy and completeness across large historical datasets often benefits from the thorough data cleaning, validation, and reconciliation processes that are characteristic of batch processing. Finally, for certain workloads where latency requirements are less stringent, cost optimization can often be achieved through the efficient resource utilization and scheduling capabilities of batch processing.

Hybrid architectures prove beneficial in scenarios that necessitate a blend of the strengths offered by both real-time and batch processing. When both real-time and historical views are required, such as applications that need to display immediate operational metrics alongside long-term performance trends or provide real-time alerts based on deviations from historical patterns, a hybrid approach that merges data from both processing paths offers a comprehensive solution. Similarly, when there's a need for balancing latency and accuracy, where near-real-time insights are valuable for immediate action, but a more accurate and comprehensive historical view is also essential for in-depth analysis and strategic decision-making, a hybrid architecture can strike the right balance. Furthermore, organizations may strategically adopt a Lambda architecture as a gradual transition to real-time processing, allowing them to build out real-time capabilities while still leveraging their existing batch processing infrastructure and expertise. The choice of architecture in these hybrid scenarios often involves carefully considering the specific latency requirements for different aspects of the application, the desired level of accuracy for both real-time and historical data, and the complexity and cost associated with maintaining multiple processing pipelines. Ultimately, the strategic selection hinges on a deep understanding of the use case's needs and the inherent trade-offs between the temporal characteristics, processing capabilities, and operational complexities of real-time, batch, and hybrid approaches.

Optimizing Batch Processing: The Power of Incremental Processing

To address the inherent latency associated with processing massive historical datasets in batch, a suite of techniques known as incremental processing has emerged as a powerful optimization strategy. Instead of the resource-intensive approach of reprocessing the entire dataset with each batch job execution, incremental processing intelligently focuses computational efforts solely on the new data that has arrived or the data that has changed since the last successful processing cycle. This targeted approach yields significant reductions in both processing time and overall resource consumption for batch workloads, making the analysis of large historical datasets more agile and cost-effective.

One key technique for achieving incremental processing is Watermarking. This involves tracking the progress of data processing based on timestamps associated with the events themselves. By maintaining a "watermark," which represents the point in time up to which data has been successfully processed in the previous run, subsequent batch jobs can efficiently identify and process only the data with timestamps occurring after this watermark. This method is particularly effective for time-series data or event logs where the order and timestamp of events are crucial for tracking progress.

Another powerful approach is Change Data Capture (CDC). CDC focuses on identifying and extracting only the data that has been created, updated, or deleted in the source systems since the last data extraction. This eliminates the need to scan and compare entire datasets to identify changes. Various CDC mechanisms exist, including database transaction logs, triggers, and specialized CDC tools that monitor data modifications at the source level. By processing only the changes, CDC significantly reduces the volume of data that needs to be processed in each batch cycle.

Delta Processing offers another strategy for incremental updates. This technique involves comparing the current state of the data with the previous state and processing only the differences or "delta" between the two. This might involve identifying new records, modified records, or deleted records. Delta processing often requires maintaining a snapshot or a historical record of the data's previous state to perform the comparison. While effective for reducing the processing load, implementing delta processing can introduce complexity in managing and comparing data states.

Maintaining Consistency Across Real-Time and Batch Paradigms

Ensuring data consistency across systems that employ both real-time and batch processing presents a significant architectural challenge, particularly in hybrid models like the Lambda architecture, where data traverses two distinct processing pathways. Discrepancies between the near real-time view provided by the speed layer and the eventually consistent view offered by the batch layer can lead to confusion and undermine the reliability of the overall data platform. Several strategies can be employed to mitigate these consistency challenges.

Designing processing logic in both the real-time and batch layers to be idempotent operations is a crucial step. Idempotency ensures that reprocessing the same data multiple times, whether due to retries or the inherent nature of dual-path processing, produces the same final result without any unintended side effects or data duplication. This requires careful consideration of how each processing step handles data updates and transformations.

Defining a consistent data model that is adhered to across both processing pipelines is essential for ensuring a unified interpretation of the data. Regardless of whether data is processed in real-time or in batch, the underlying structure, data types, and semantics should remain consistent.

This reduces the likelihood of misinterpretations and facilitates seamless merging of data from the two layers in the serving layer.

Implementing Data Versioning provides a mechanism for tracking and managing different versions of data as it progresses through both the real-time and batch processing layers. This allows for auditing changes, understanding the lineage of data transformations, and potentially resolving inconsistencies by referring to specific data versions.

Establishing reconciliation processes involves periodically comparing and reconciling the data produced by the real-time and batch layers. These processes can identify any discrepancies that may have arisen due to differences in processing logic, timing, or failures. Once discrepancies are identified, mechanisms need to be in place to investigate the root causes and resolve them, ensuring the overall consistency of the data presented to the end users.

Aiming to utilize a single source of truth is a fundamental principle for maximizing data consistency. This involves designating a single, authoritative data store that serves as the foundation for both real-time and batch processing. By having both pipelines read from and potentially write back to this central store (or derived views of it), the risk of inconsistencies arising from disparate data sources is significantly reduced. This approach often aligns well with the principles of the Kappa architecture, where a single, immutable stream of events serves as the source of truth for all processing.

By strategically employing incremental processing techniques to optimize batch workloads and diligently implementing consistency management strategies across real-time and batch paradigms, organizations can build robust and reliable data platforms that effectively leverage the strengths of both approaches while mitigating their inherent challenges. This careful balancing act is crucial for achieving optimal data utilization and delivering accurate, timely insights from petabyte-scale datasets.

Strategically Navigating the Temporal Landscape of Data Processing

Strategically navigating the temporal landscape of data processing, encompassing the deliberate choice between real-time and batch methodologies and the thoughtful adoption of hybrid architectures, stands as a pivotal decision in the design and implementation of efficient and effective petabyte-scale data platforms. This selection is not merely a technical consideration but a strategic imperative that directly impacts an organization's ability to derive timely, accurate, and comprehensive value from its vast data assets. A deep understanding of the inherent trade-offs associated with each processing paradigm – encompassing latency, architectural complexity, operational cost, and the scope of analytical capabilities – is absolutely paramount for making informed decisions.

The choice between the immediacy of real-time processing and the thoroughness of batch processing, or the synergistic combination offered by hybrid architectures, must be meticulously aligned with the specific requirements and objectives of each individual use case. Applications demanding instant responsiveness to incoming events, such as fraud detection or real-time anomaly identification, unequivocally necessitate the low latency and continuous nature of real-time processing. Conversely, use cases focused on in-depth historical analysis, complex transformations across entire datasets, or ensuring the highest levels of data accuracy and completeness often find batch processing to be the more suitable and efficient approach.

Recognizing the limitations of a purely one-sided approach, the strategic adoption of hybrid architectures like Lambda and Kappa offers a pragmatic path towards building comprehensive data platforms that can cater to a wider spectrum of analytical and operational needs. These architectures acknowledge the complementary strengths of both real-time and batch processing, enabling organizations to leverage the low latency of stream processing for immediate insights while still harnessing the power of batch processing for deep historical analysis and data integrity. The careful consideration of the trade-offs inherent in each hybrid model, particularly regarding complexity and the burden placed on the underlying processing infrastructure, is crucial for successful implementation.

Additionally, the optimization of batch processing through the implementation of incremental processing techniques becomes increasingly vital at petabyte scale. By focusing computational resources only on new or changed data, organizations can significantly mitigate the latency traditionally associated with batch workloads, making the analysis of massive historical datasets more agile and responsive. Techniques like watermarking, Change Data Capture (CDC), and delta processing represent powerful tools in this optimization endeavor.

The challenge of maintaining data consistency across systems that employ different temporal processing layers, especially in hybrid architectures, demands careful consideration and the implementation of robust strategies. Techniques such as designing idempotent operations, enforcing consistent data models across pipelines, implementing data versioning, establishing reconciliation processes, and striving for a single source of truth are essential for ensuring the reliability and trustworthiness of the data presented to end users and applications.

In conclusion, the ability to strategically navigate this temporal landscape of data processing to thoughtfully select the appropriate processing paradigm for each use case, to optimize batch workloads for greater efficiency, and to ensure data consistency across disparate temporal layers is not merely a technical skill but a hallmark of a mature and agile data-driven organization. It reflects a deep understanding of the organization's data assets, its analytical and operational needs, and the capabilities and limitations of various data processing technologies. By mastering this strategic navigation, organizations can unlock the full potential of their vast data assets, gaining both immediate competitive advantages through real-time insights and long-term strategic understanding through comprehensive historical analysis, ultimately fostering a truly data-driven culture and achieving sustained success in an increasingly data-centric world.

CHAPTER NINE

SECURITY AND GOVERNANCE IN LARGE-SCALE PIPELINES

The transition to managing data at petabyte scale dramatically elevates the stakes associated with both security and governance. The sheer magnitude of information concentrated within these systems transforms them into highly lucrative targets for malicious actors. A successful security breach in a petabyte-scale environment can expose unprecedented volumes of sensitive data, potentially encompassing personal information, financial records, intellectual property, and strategic business intelligence. The consequences of such an incident are not merely incremental; they are exponentially amplified, potentially leading to catastrophic financial losses through fines, legal settlements, and recovery costs; irreparable reputational damage eroding customer trust and brand value; and severe legal repercussions stemming from regulatory non-compliance.

Furthermore, the inherent complexity of large-scale, distributed data pipelines characteristic of petabyte-scale environments significantly broadens the attack surface. These pipelines often involve numerous interconnected systems, diverse data sources with varying security postures, and a multitude of access points. Each component and connection represents a potential vulnerability that, if exploited, could provide a gateway for unauthorized access, data exfiltration, or malicious manipulation. Vigilant and comprehensive protection across this expanded attack surface is therefore paramount, requiring a multi-layered security strategy that addresses every stage of the data lifecycle.

Similarly, effective data governance undergoes a significant transformation in terms of both challenge and criticality as data proliferates across the organization at petabyte scale. The sheer volume and variety of data, often residing in disparate systems and subject to diverse processing workflows, can easily lead to data silos, inconsistencies in data quality, and a lack of a unified understanding of the organization's information assets. Without clearly defined policies and robust processes for managing data access, usage, quality control, and lifecycle management, organizations risk severe compliance violations with increasingly stringent data privacy regulations, ethical breaches in data utilization, and a fundamental lack of trust in the data itself, hindering effective decision-making and analytical insights.

Establishing robust governance frameworks becomes not merely a best practice but a fundamental necessity for navigating the complexities of petabyte-scale data. These frameworks must ensure that data is accurate, reliable, consistently defined, and used ethically and in accordance with all applicable regulatory requirements. This includes implementing clear data ownership and stewardship, defining data quality standards and monitoring processes, establishing comprehensive data access controls and audit trails, and implementing policies for data retention and disposal.

Therefore, in the petabyte era, security and governance can no longer be treated as afterthoughts or bolted-on components. They must be considered foundational pillars in the very design and operation of petabyte-scale data platforms, seamlessly integrated into every stage of the data lifecycle, from the initial ingestion of raw data to its eventual consumption for analytical or operational purposes. A piecemeal or reactive approach to security and governance is simply insufficient and dangerously inadequate in the face of the immense scale and intricate complexity involved. A proactive, holistic, and deeply embedded approach is essential to mitigate the heightened risks and ensure the responsible and secure management of these invaluable data assets. This requires a shift in mindset, viewing security and governance not as impediments but as enablers of trust, compliance, and ultimately, the long-term value derived from petabyte-scale data.

Securing the Data Fortress: Encryption and Access Control at Scale

In the realm of petabyte-scale data, the sheer volume and potential sensitivity of the information necessitate a robust and comprehensive security posture. Two foundational pillars of this security fortress are encryption and access control, both of which must be implemented with meticulous attention to detail and designed to scale effectively alongside the ever-expanding data landscape.

Encryption serves as a fundamental security imperative by rendering data unintelligible to unauthorized parties. It acts as a crucial last line of defense in the event of a security breach, ensuring that even if malicious actors gain access to the storage infrastructure or data streams, the information remains confidential and unusable without the correct decryption keys.

Encryption at rest focuses on protecting data while it is stored on persistent storage mediums. This encompasses a wide range of storage solutions prevalent in petabyte-scale environments, including distributed file systems like HDFS, NoSQL databases such as Cassandra or MongoDB, data warehouses like Snowflake or Redshift, and object storage services like Amazon S3 or Azure Blob Storage. Employing strong encryption algorithms, such as AES-256, is paramount for ensuring the confidentiality of the stored data. Equally critical is the implementation of robust key management systems. These systems are responsible for securely generating, storing, distributing, rotating, and revoking encryption keys. Weak key management can undermine the effectiveness of even the strongest encryption algorithms. Scalable key management solutions that can handle a vast number of keys and integrate seamlessly with distributed storage systems are essential in petabyte-scale deployments.

Encryption in transit addresses the vulnerability of data as it moves between different components of the data pipeline. This includes data being ingested from source systems, processed by various compute engines, and served to downstream applications or users. Utilizing secure communication protocols like Transport Layer Security (TLS) and its predecessor, Secure Sockets Layer (SSL) is crucial for establishing encrypted channels between these components. This prevents eavesdropping, where unauthorized parties intercept data as it travels across the network, and protects against data interception or tampering during transmission. Ensuring that all internal and external communication within the data platform leverages strong encryption in transit is a non-negotiable security requirement at petabyte scale.

Access Control: Granting Entry with Precision

While encryption provides a protective shield around the data itself, access control mechanisms are equally vital for ensuring that only authorized users and applications can access specific data assets and perform designated actions upon them. This principle of least privilege, granting users only the minimum level of access necessary to perform their assigned tasks, is a cornerstone of secure data management.

Implementing fine-grained access control involves defining roles and permissions at a granular level, often down to specific datasets, tables, columns, or even individual records. This allows for precise control over who can view, modify, or delete data. Role-Based Access Control (RBAC) is a common model where permissions are associated with roles, and users are assigned to these roles based on their job functions or responsibilities.

Attribute-Based Access Control (ABAC) offers a more dynamic and context-aware approach, where access decisions are based on attributes of the user, the resource being accessed, and the environment.

The Cornerstone of Control: Metadata Management

In the sprawling landscape of petabyte-scale data, where information proliferates across diverse systems and undergoes complex transformations, effective metadata management emerges as the paramount cornerstone of control. Without a robust and comprehensive understanding of the data itself its origins, characteristics, relationships, and usage organizations risk being overwhelmed by a chaotic sea of information, unable to govern it effectively, secure it adequately, or derive meaningful insights with confidence. Metadata, often described as "data about data," provides the crucial context necessary to navigate this complexity, acting as the indispensable map and compass for the vast data terrain.

At its core, metadata management encompasses the processes and technologies involved in creating, capturing, storing, managing, and utilizing metadata. This includes a wide array of information about data assets, such as their origin (where did the data come from?), format (is it structured, semi-structured, or unstructured?), schema (what is the structure and organization of the data?), quality (what are the data quality metrics and profiles?), ownership (who is responsible for this data?), and usage (how is this data being used?).

A centralized metadata catalog serves as the linchpin of effective metadata management in petabyte-scale environments. This catalog acts as a single, authoritative repository, a "single source of truth" for all data assets residing within the platform. By consolidating metadata from disparate systems and providing a unified view, the catalog enables several critical capabilities. Firstly, it facilitates data discovery, allowing users and applications to easily find the data they need based on various criteria, such as keywords, data types, or business domains. This eliminates the costly and time-consuming process of manually searching for and understanding data scattered across different silos.

Secondly, a centralized metadata catalog is instrumental in understanding data relationships. By capturing information about data lineage (the journey of data from its source to its final destination), data dependencies (how different datasets are related), and data transformations (the processes data undergoes), the catalog provides a holistic view of how data flows and interacts within the platform. This understanding is crucial for impact analysis, troubleshooting data quality issues, and ensuring the integrity of analytical pipelines.

Thirdly, and perhaps most critically, effective metadata management is essential for enforcing data governance policies. The metadata catalog provides the necessary context to apply rules and regulations related to data access, usage, quality, and lifecycle management. For instance, policies regarding data sensitivity can be linked to metadata tags, enabling automated enforcement of access controls and masking rules. Similarly, data retention policies can be applied based on metadata indicating the data's age and purpose.

Furthermore, comprehensive metadata management is a prerequisite for implementing effective access control. By understanding the sensitivity and classification of data through its metadata, organizations can apply granular access policies, ensuring that only authorized users and applications can access specific data assets. The metadata catalog can be integrated with identity management systems to enforce these policies consistently across the entire data platform.

Tracking data lineage, a key aspect of metadata management, is crucial for ensuring data quality and compliance. By understanding the complete history of a data asset, from its origin through all its transformations, organizations can trace back errors, identify potential data quality issues, and demonstrate compliance with regulatory requirements that mandate data provenance.

The sheer volume and complexity of metadata associated with petabyte-scale data necessitate scalable metadata platforms that can handle this immense load efficiently. These platforms must be able to ingest metadata from a multitude of sources, store it reliably, provide efficient querying and search capabilities, and integrate with other data management and security tools. The ability to automatically discover and classify metadata is also increasingly important in managing the vast and ever-growing data landscape.

In the petabyte era, metadata management is not merely a supporting function; it is the very cornerstone of control. It provides the essential context for understanding, governing, and securing the organization's most valuable asset – its data. A centralized, scalable, and comprehensive metadata management system is indispensable for enabling data discovery, understanding data relationships, enforcing governance policies, implementing effective access control, tracking data lineage, and ultimately, unlocking the full potential of petabyte-scale data while mitigating the significant risks associated with its scale and complexity.

Tracing the Data Journey: Data Lineage Tracking

Data lineage tracking provides a comprehensive audit trail of how data flows through the ingestion, processing, and storage stages of the data pipeline. It maps the origin of data, the transformations it undergoes, and its ultimate destination. Understanding data lineage is critical for several reasons: it enables tracing the root cause of data quality issues, facilitates impact analysis when changes are made to the data pipeline, supports regulatory compliance by demonstrating data provenance, and aids in security investigations by tracking data access and movement. At petabyte scale, lineage tracking systems must be able to handle the vast number of metadata generated by complex data flows without introducing significant performance overhead.

Ensuring Accountability: Auditing Techniques at Scale

By meticulously recording a comprehensive history of interactions with data and the systems that manage it, auditing provides an indispensable trail for understanding data access patterns, detecting suspicious activities, facilitating incident response, and meeting stringent regulatory requirements. The sheer volume and velocity of operations within petabyte-scale environments, however, necessitate the deployment of sophisticated and scalable auditing techniques.

Comprehensive audit logging forms the foundation of effective accountability. This involves capturing a wide spectrum of events, including detailed records of who accessed what data, specifying the user or application involved and the particular data assets targeted. The audit logs must also record when these access attempts occurred, providing a precise temporal context for every interaction. Furthermore, logging what actions were performed is critical, detailing whether data was viewed, modified, created, deleted, or if system configurations were altered or security-related events transpired. The level of detail captured in these audit logs should be granular enough to provide meaningful insights without overwhelming the system with extraneous information.

The immense scale of petabyte environments invariably leads to a high volume of audit logs. Every data access, every query, every system change across a vast distributed infrastructure can generate audit records. Traditional, centralized logging mechanisms often struggle to cope with this deluge of information, potentially leading to performance bottlenecks, data loss, and difficulties in analysis. Therefore, scalable audit logging systems are paramount. These systems must be designed to handle the continuous influx of audit data without impacting the performance or stability of the core data platform. Distributed logging architectures, leveraging technologies capable of high-throughput ingestion and storage, are often employed.

Once the audit logs are generated and stored, efficient storage, indexing, and querying capabilities become essential for their effective utilization. Raw audit logs, especially at petabyte scale, can be unwieldy and difficult to analyze. Efficient storage solutions, often involving distributed storage clusters optimized for write-heavy workloads, are necessary to accommodate the sheer volume. Robust indexing mechanisms are crucial for enabling rapid retrieval of specific audit records based on various criteria, such as user ID, accessed data asset, timestamp, or action performed. Finally, powerful querying capabilities are needed to perform complex analysis, identify patterns, and correlate events across the vast audit log data.

To manage and analyze audit logs at scale effectively, several techniques and technologies are commonly employed. Log aggregation involves consolidating logs from numerous distributed systems into a central repository, simplifying management and analysis. Centralized log management platforms provide tools for storing, organizing, and searching these aggregated logs. Security Information and Event Management (SIEM) systems take this a step further by collecting and analyzing security-related logs from various sources across the IT infrastructure, including audit logs from the data platform. SIEM systems can perform real-time analysis, correlate events, identify potential security threats, and generate alerts, providing crucial capabilities for security monitoring and incident response in petabyte-scale environments.

Auditing at petabyte scale is not a mere compliance checkbox; it is a fundamental security and governance control that provides essential accountability. Scalable audit logging systems, coupled with efficient storage, indexing, and querying capabilities, and often leveraging log aggregation, centralized log management, and SIEM technologies, are crucial for navigating the complexities of these vast data landscapes. By providing a detailed and auditable record of data interactions and system activities, organizations can effectively monitor their security posture, respond swiftly to incidents, demonstrate compliance with regulations, and ultimately build trust in the integrity and security of their petabyte-scale data fortress.

Balancing Security and Performance: A Delicate Act

Implementing robust security and governance measures in petabyte-scale pipelines requires a careful balancing act with performance considerations. Encryption and fine-grained access control can introduce computational overhead. Metadata management and lineage tracking can generate significant metadata that needs to be stored and queried efficiently. Auditing can produce vast amounts of log data that need to be managed without impacting pipeline performance. Therefore, architectural choices must consider security and governance requirements from the outset, and optimization techniques may be necessary to minimize the performance impact of these essential controls. This includes leveraging hardware acceleration for encryption, optimizing metadata storage and retrieval, and employing efficient log processing and analysis techniques

Securing and governing petabyte-scale data pipelines is not merely a technical challenge; it is a fundamental responsibility that underpins trust, compliance, and the ethical use of data. By implementing robust encryption, fine-grained access control, and adhering to data privacy regulations, organizations can protect their valuable data assets and the privacy of their users. Comprehensive metadata management, data lineage tracking, and effective auditing techniques provide the necessary visibility and accountability to ensure data quality, compliance, and security throughout the data lifecycle. As organizations navigate the ever-expanding ocean of data, a proactive and integrated approach to security and governance is essential for harnessing its power responsibly and sustainably.

Ensuring Accountability: Auditing Techniques at Scale

Security measures, by their very nature, frequently introduce overhead and can potentially impact the speed and efficiency of data processing and access. Conversely, prioritizing performance without adequate security controls can expose vast amounts of sensitive data to significant risks. Therefore, a thoughtful and strategic approach is essential to navigate this tension, ensuring a secure yet performant environment.

The inherent trade-offs between security and performance manifest in various aspects of petabyte-scale data management. For instance, encryption, a cornerstone of data protection, adds computational overhead during both the encryption and decryption processes. While crucial for safeguarding data at rest and in transit, employing strong encryption algorithms and complex key management can potentially increase latency and consume processing resources. Similarly, fine-grained access control mechanisms, while essential for enforcing the principle of least privilege, can introduce complexity in authorization checks, potentially adding overhead to data access requests, especially when dealing with a large number of users, roles, and data assets.

Auditing, another vital security and compliance measure, involves logging detailed information about data access and system activities. While crucial for accountability and threat detection, the continuous writing and management of voluminous audit logs in petabyte-scale environments can consume storage resources and potentially impact write performance if not implemented efficiently. Network security measures, such as intrusion detection and prevention systems, while critical for protecting the data platform from external threats, can also introduce latency as network traffic is inspected and analyzed.

The challenge lies in implementing security controls in a manner that minimizes their impact on performance without compromising their effectiveness. This requires a deep understanding of both the security risks and the performance requirements of the specific use cases and workloads running on the petabyte-scale platform. A one-size-fits-all approach is rarely effective; instead, a nuanced and context-aware strategy is necessary.

Several key principles and techniques can help organizations strike this delicate balance. Risk-based security is paramount, focusing the most stringent security controls on the most sensitive data and critical systems. This allows for a more pragmatic allocation of security resources and minimizes unnecessary overhead on less sensitive data or less critical workflows. Optimizing security implementations is also crucial. For example, selecting encryption algorithms that offer a strong security-performance trade-off, leveraging hardware acceleration for cryptographic operations, and implementing efficient key management strategies can help mitigate the performance impact of encryption. Similarly, designing scalable and efficient access control mechanisms, such as leveraging caching for authorization decisions and optimizing policy enforcement engines, can minimize overhead.

Architectural considerations play a significant role in balancing security and performance. Designing data pipelines and storage systems with security in mind from the outset, a principle known as "security by design," can often lead to more efficient and less intrusive security implementations. For instance, partitioning data based on sensitivity can allow for the application of different security controls to different segments, optimizing both security and performance. Utilizing distributed and parallel processing architectures can help offset the performance overhead introduced by security measures by distributing the workload across multiple nodes.

Continuous monitoring and optimization are also essential. Regularly assessing the performance impact of security controls and fine-tuning their configurations can help identify and address potential bottlenecks. Security monitoring tools can also help detect anomalies that might indicate both security breaches and performance issues, allowing for timely intervention.

Furthermore, the choice of technology can significantly influence the balance between security and performance. Some data processing and storage technologies offer built-in security features that are designed to be performant on a scale. Evaluating these options carefully and selecting technologies that align with both security and performance requirements is crucial.

Balancing security and performance in petabyte-scale data platforms is not a static state but an ongoing process of assessment, optimization, and adaptation. It requires a strategic mindset that prioritizes risk mitigation while remaining acutely aware of the performance implications of security controls. By adopting a risk-based approach, optimizing security implementations, considering architectural implications, embracing continuous monitoring, and making informed technology choices, organizations can strive to build secure and performant data fortresses that can effectively handle the challenges and opportunities of the petabyte era.

Securing and governing petabyte-scale data pipelines transcends the realm of purely technical challenges; it embodies a fundamental responsibility that underpins the very foundations of trust, ensures adherence to legal and ethical obligations, and fosters the sustainable and ethical utilization of data. In an era where data has become a ubiquitous and invaluable resource, the manner in which organizations manage and protect these vast digital oceans directly impacts their reputation, their legal standing, and their relationship with users and stakeholders.

Implementing robust encryption mechanisms, both at rest and in transit, forms a critical layer of defense against unauthorized access and potential data breaches. By rendering data unintelligible to malicious actors, encryption safeguards sensitive information and upholds the privacy of individuals whose data may be contained within these massive datasets. Coupled with fine-grained access control systems, which meticulously regulate who can access specific data assets and what actions they are permitted to perform, organizations can establish a secure perimeter around their data fortress, minimizing the risk of internal and external threats. Adhering to evolving data privacy regulations, such as GDPR, CCPA, and others, is not just a matter of legal compliance but a demonstration of ethical data stewardship, ensuring that individuals' rights to privacy and control over their personal information are respected.

Comprehensive metadata management serves as the indispensable compass for navigating the complexities of petabyte-scale data. By providing crucial context about data assets – their origin, format, quality, ownership, and usage – metadata enables organizations to understand their data landscape, facilitate data discovery, and enforce governance policies effectively. Tracking data lineage, the detailed journey of data from its source through all its transformations, provides the necessary visibility to ensure data quality, trace errors, and demonstrate compliance with regulations requiring data provenance. Effective auditing techniques, which meticulously record who accessed what data, when, and what actions were performed, establish the necessary accountability to monitor data usage, detect suspicious activities, and respond swiftly to security incidents.

As organizations increasingly navigate the ever-expanding ocean of data, a proactive and integrated approach to security and governance is not merely advisable; it is absolutely essential for harnessing its immense power responsibly and sustainably. A reactive or piecemeal approach, where security and governance are treated as afterthoughts, is simply insufficient to address the scale and complexity of petabyte-scale data and the potential ramifications of security breaches or governance lapses. Instead, security and governance must be woven into the very fabric of the data platform, considered at every stage of the data lifecycle, from initial ingestion to final consumption. This requires a cultural shift within the organization, fostering a mindset where data security and responsible data handling are not just tasks for a dedicated team but shared responsibilities across all data stakeholders.

By embracing this proactive and integrated approach, organizations can build data platforms that are not only powerful and scalable but also trustworthy and ethically sound. This responsible governance of the data ocean fosters user confidence, ensures compliance with legal obligations, protects valuable data assets, and ultimately enables organizations to leverage the full potential of their data in a sustainable and ethical manner, building a future where data empowers progress without compromising security or privacy.

CHAPTER TEN

FUTURE-PROOFING YOUR DATA INFRASTRUCTURE

T he intricate and often challenging journey through the construction and management of petabyte scale data platforms, as detailed in the preceding chapters, has illuminated the immense power and equally significant complexities inherent in handling such colossal volumes of information. However, it is crucial to recognize that the current technological landscape, characterized by the management of data in petabyte quantities and a dominant paradigm of centralized cloud-based processing, represents merely a significant, yet ultimately transitional, phase in the ongoing and relentless evolution of data infrastructure. The future, poised on the cusp of groundbreaking technological advancements, promises even more profound and potentially transformative shifts in how we approach the fundamental processes of data collection, storage, processing, and the extraction of meaningful insights. This final chapter embarks on an ambitious exploration of these nascent yet potentially revolutionary trends, venturing into the uncharted territories of the proliferating realm of edge computing, the collaborative and privacy-preserving power of federated learning methodologies, and the tantalizing, albeit still largely theoretical, possibilities presented by the burgeoning field of quantum data storage. Our ultimate aim is to provide a strategic and forward-looking roadmap for building inherently adaptable data pipelines – architectures that are not only equipped to handle the escalating demands of tomorrow's data landscape, characterized by exabyte and beyond scales, but are also intrinsically designed with the flexibility and agility to evolve seamlessly alongside these anticipated technological advancements. This proactive approach will be paramount in ensuring long-term scalability, sustained operational efficiency, and a continued, unimpeded ability to unlock invaluable knowledge and drive innovation from the ever-expanding and increasingly complex universe of data.

The Evolving Dataverse: Dissecting the Emerging Trends That Will Fundamentally Reshape Future Infrastructure

The global data landscape is not a static entity; rather, it exists in a perpetual state of dynamic flux, driven by the relentless pace of innovation across a diverse spectrum of technological domains. For organizations striving to maintain a competitive edge and harness the full potential of their data assets in the long term, a deep understanding and proactive strategic preparation for these emerging trends are not merely advisable but represent a fundamental imperative for building data infrastructure that remains relevant, efficient, and capable of adapting to the inevitable shifts in the technological landscape.

The Decentralized Frontier: The Paradigm Shift of Edge Computing

The traditional, and currently dominant, model of centralized data processing, primarily anchored in the vast computational resources of cloud-based platforms, is facing an increasing challenge and a significant paradigm shift with the rapid ascent and widespread adoption of edge computing. This transformative paradigm fundamentally alters the locus of data processing, advocating for the execution of computational tasks closer to the actual source of data generation – whether that source be a myriad of interconnected devices, a dense network of industrial sensors, or local, on-premises servers situated at the periphery of the network. This distributed approach to data processing offers a constellation of compelling advantages that directly address some of the inherent limitations of centralized cloud models. These benefits include a dramatic reduction in latency, which is critical for real-time applications demanding immediate responsiveness (e.g., autonomous vehicles, industrial control systems, augmented reality); a significant decrease in the consumption of network bandwidth by processing and filtering data locally before transmitting only essential information to the cloud; enhanced data privacy and security by keeping sensitive data within local environments and minimizing its exposure during transit; and improved operational resilience, particularly in environments characterized by intermittent or unreliable network connectivity, where local processing can continue uninterrupted. As the Internet of Things (IoT) continues its exponential proliferation, generating unprecedented volumes of data at the very edge of networks, future data infrastructures will necessitate the seamless and intelligent integration of edge processing capabilities. This will involve enabling sophisticated data filtering, real-time preprocessing, and even the deployment and execution of machine learning inference models directly on edge devices or local edge servers. This distributed processing model will require the development of novel architectural patterns for data ingestion, distributed storage management, and efficient model deployment and updating across the vast and heterogeneous landscape spanning from resource-constrained edge devices to powerful centralized cloud platforms.

Collaborative Intelligence: Unleashing the Power of Federated Learning

The conventional approach to training machine learning models often relies on the centralization of massive datasets into a single, unified location. While this strategy has proven effective in many scenarios, it can raise significant concerns regarding data privacy, particularly when dealing with sensitive user information or proprietary organizational data. Furthermore, this centralized approach may not be practically feasible when data is inherently distributed across a vast network of decentralized devices (e.g., smartphones, medical sensors) or across the data silos of multiple independent organizations. Federated learning emerges as a revolutionary and privacy-preserving alternative, enabling collaborative training of robust machine learning models across a distributed network of devices or servers without ever requiring the sharing or aggregation of the raw, underlying data itself. Instead of transmitting sensitive data to a central server, individual devices or local servers train their own local models based on their locally held data. Only the learned model updates – such as gradients or model parameters – are then selectively aggregated at a central server to create a more generalized and globally effective model. This innovative approach inherently preserves data privacy and enhances data security by keeping the raw data decentralized and protected at its source. Moreover, it unlocks the immense potential for training highly accurate and robust machine learning models on massive, geographically distributed datasets that would otherwise be inaccessible due to privacy regulations, data ownership restrictions, or logistical challenges. Future data infrastructures will need to seamlessly incorporate frameworks, tools, and standardized protocols that facilitate efficient and secure federated learning workflows, enabling the development of collaborative intelligence while rigorously respecting data sovereignty, user privacy, and organizational data governance policies.

The Quantum Leap: Exploring the Transformative Potential of Quantum Data Storage

While still residing primarily in the realm of theoretical research and early-stage development, the burgeoning field of quantum computing holds the potential to fundamentally revolutionize various aspects of information technology, including the very nature of data storage. Quantum data storage leverages the unique and counterintuitive principles of quantum mechanics, such as superposition and entanglement, to store and retrieve information in fundamentally different ways compared to classical storage technologies that rely on binary bits representing 0s and 1s. While the realization of practical, fault-tolerant quantum computers and scalable quantum memory remains a significant scientific and engineering challenge that is likely to take years, if not decades, to overcome, the theoretical possibilities offered by quantum storage are truly immense. Quantum storage could potentially offer exponentially higher data storage densities, allowing for the storage of vastly greater amounts of information in significantly smaller physical spaces. Furthermore, the unique properties of quantum mechanics could potentially lead to unprecedentedly faster data access and retrieval speeds. While the widespread and practical adoption of quantum data storage is still a long-term prospect, organizations with a long-term strategic vision for their data infrastructure should begin to actively monitor advancements in the field of quantum computing and explore potential integration pathways and architectural implications as the underlying technology matures and becomes more commercially viable. Understanding the long-term potential of quantum storage will be crucial for making informed decisions about future infrastructure investments and ensuring that data platforms are positioned to leverage these transformative capabilities when they eventually become available.

Building Adaptable Pipelines: A Strategic Roadmap for Future Scalability and Sustained Efficiency

To ensure the long-term scalability, sustained operational efficiency, and continued value extraction from data in the face of these rapidly evolving technological landscapes, organizations must adopt a proactive, flexible, and inherently adaptable approach to the design and construction of their data infrastructure:

Embrace Hybrid and Multi-Cloud Strategies as the New Norm: The future of data infrastructure is increasingly likely to be characterized by heterogeneous environments that seamlessly blend on-premises infrastructure with the vast array of resources offered by cloud computing platforms, as well as strategic multi-cloud deployments that leverage the specialized services and unique advantages provided by different cloud vendors. Building data pipelines that possess the inherent ability to operate fluidly and efficiently across these diverse and distributed environments, with a strong emphasis on interoperability and data portability as fundamental design principles, will be absolutely crucial for maximizing flexibility, mitigating the risks of vendor lock-in, and optimizing cost and performance based on the specific requirements of different workloads.

Design for Seamless Interoperability and Adherence to Open Standards: Designing for seamless interoperability and adherence to open standards is a strategic imperative in the rapidly evolving landscape of data science and engineering, particularly when building and maintaining petabyte-scale data platforms. Favoring the adoption of open standards and embracing technologies that prioritize seamless interoperability acts as a crucial catalyst for easier integration with the constantly emerging ecosystem of new tools and platforms. In a field characterized by rapid innovation and the proliferation of specialized solutions, the ability for different systems and components to communicate and exchange data effortlessly is paramount for agility, scalability, and avoiding vendor lock-in. By strategically adopting standardized data formats, such as Parquet or Avro for efficient data storage and exchange, organizations can significantly reduce the complexities associated with data conversion and ensure broader compatibility across various processing engines and storage solutions. Similarly, well-defined application programming interfaces

(APIs), built upon open specifications like REST or GraphQL, provide clear and consistent interfaces for different applications and services to interact with each other, abstracting away underlying implementation details and facilitating smoother integration. Embracing widely accepted communication protocols, such as HTTP/HTTPS for web-based interactions or message queuing protocols like Kafka or AMQP for asynchronous data exchange, further enhances the ability of diverse systems to connect and share information reliably and efficiently. This commitment to open standards and interoperability effectively reduces the friction and complexity often encountered when incorporating novel technologies into existing data pipelines, allowing organizations to readily adopt cutting-edge tools and functionalities without being constrained by proprietary formats or incompatible interfaces. The result is a more flexible and adaptable data architecture, capable of evolving alongside the technological landscape and enabling smoother and more efficient data exchange across a diverse range of interconnected systems, ultimately fostering innovation and maximizing the value derived from data.

Cultivate Modular and Decoupled Architectures for Enhanced Agility

Building data pipelines based on modular and loosely coupled architectural principles, where individual components can be independently scaled based on demand, updated with new functionalities without impacting other parts of the system, and even replaced with newer, more efficient technologies as they become available, will be paramount for enhancing overall adaptability and resilience. Embracing microservices-based architectures and establishing well-defined and stable APIs between different data processing and storage components will promote greater flexibility, improve system maintainability, and facilitate smoother evolution in response to technological advancements.

Invest Proactively in Robust Data Governance and Comprehensive Metadata Management

Investing proactively in robust data governance and comprehensive Metadata management is not merely a prudent measure but a fundamental necessity for organizations navigating the increasingly complex and distributed data landscape of the future. As data generation expands beyond centralized data lakes to encompass edge devices, as collaborative learning paradigms like federated learning gain prominence, and as potentially revolutionary storage technologies such as quantum storage emerge, the challenges of understanding, trusting, and responsibly utilizing data will only intensify. A strong and well-established foundation of data governance principles will provide the overarching framework for defining data ownership, establishing data quality standards, enforcing data security policies, and ensuring compliance with evolving regulatory landscapes across these diverse environments. Without clear guidelines and accountability structures, the distributed nature of future data ecosystems could easily lead to data silos, inconsistencies, and a lack of trust in the veracity and reliability of information. Complementing this governance foundation, a comprehensive and actively maintained metadata management system will become even more critical. This system will serve as the central nervous system for understanding the lineage of data – tracing its origins, transformations, and destinations across edge devices, federated learning participants, and novel storage systems. It will provide crucial visibility into data quality metrics, enabling organizations to assess the reliability and suitability of data for specific analytical tasks, regardless of its physical location. Furthermore, metadata management will be essential for maintaining security and compliance classifications, ensuring that sensitive data is appropriately protected and that its usage adheres to relevant regulations, even as it resides in and moves through these distributed and potentially novel environments. Understanding data usage patterns across these diverse environments will also be paramount for

142

ensuring responsible and ethical data utilization, preventing misuse, and maximizing the value derived from information while respecting privacy and security boundaries. In essence, proactive investment in robust data governance and comprehensive metadata management is not just about managing data today; it is about building the essential scaffolding for navigating the complexities of tomorrow's data landscape, ensuring data trust, maintaining regulatory compliance, and enabling responsible and ethical data utilization in an increasingly distributed and technologically advanced world.

Cultivate and Nurture In-House Expertise in Emerging Technologies:

Organizations must strategically invest in developing and retaining in-house talent that possesses a deep understanding and practical skills in emerging technological domains such as edge computing architectures, federated learning frameworks, and the fundamental principles of quantum computing (at least from a strategic awareness and potential application perspective). Having a skilled workforce that can identify opportunities for the strategic adoption of these technologies and effectively integrate them into future data infrastructure will be a crucial differentiator in maintaining a competitive edge.

Embrace Infrastructure-as-Code (IaC) and Comprehensive Automation:

Embracing infrastructure-as-code (IaC) and comprehensive automation is a strategic imperative for organizations navigating the complexities of increasingly distributed and heterogeneous data environments, especially at petabyte scale. Strategically adopting IaC principles, where the entirety of the underlying infrastructure, including servers, networks, storage, and services, is defined and managed through code rather than manual configuration, offers a paradigm shift towards greater agility and control.

143

By treating infrastructure as code, organizations can leverage familiar software development practices such as version control, code reviews, and automated testing to manage their infrastructure in a consistent, repeatable, and auditable manner. This eliminates the inconsistencies and potential errors associated with manual configuration, leading to more stable and reliable data platforms. Furthermore, implementing comprehensive automation across the entire lifecycle of infrastructure encompassing provisioning new resources, deploying applications and services, scaling infrastructure up or down in response to demand, and managing ongoing maintenance tasks will be the key to efficiently deploying, scaling, and managing the ever-growing array of new and evolving technologies within the data infrastructure. Automation streamlines these processes, reducing the time and effort required for infrastructure management and freeing up valuable engineering resources to focus on higher-level data science and analytics initiatives. It enables rapid and consistent deployments, facilitates seamless scaling to accommodate fluctuating data volumes and processing demands, and ensures that infrastructure can adapt quickly to the integration of new tools and platforms. By minimizing manual intervention, automation also reduces the risk of human error, enhances security through consistent configurations, and improves overall operational efficiency. In essence, embracing IaC and comprehensive automation transforms infrastructure management from a reactive, manual burden into a proactive, code-driven capability that underpins organizational agility and effectively reduces the inherent complexity of managing increasingly distributed and heterogeneous data environments at scale.

Foster a Culture of Continuous Experimentation and Lifelong Learning:

The relentless pace of technological change within the data landscape will only continue to accelerate. To remain at the forefront of innovation, organizations must actively foster a culture of continuous experimentation and lifelong learning within their data teams. This involves encouraging exploration of new technologies, providing opportunities for skill development, and promoting a mindset of adaptability and continuous improvement in response to the evolving technological landscape.

The petabyte era, while representing a monumental achievement in our ability to manage and leverage vast quantities of data, is ultimately just one significant waypoint on the ever-evolving journey of data infrastructure. The emerging trends of edge computing, federated learning, and the long-term potential of quantum data storage signal a future that will be characterized by even greater distribution, collaboration, and potentially revolutionary advancements in storage capabilities. Future-proofing data infrastructure is not a matter of accurately predicting the precise trajectory of these nascent technologies but rather about cultivating a strategic mindset focused on building inherently adaptable, highly interoperable, and robustly governed platforms that possess the agility to evolve seamlessly alongside these inevitable advancements. By strategically embracing hybrid and multi-cloud environments, prioritizing interoperability and open standards, fostering modular and decoupled architectures, investing in strong data governance and metadata management, cultivating expertise in emerging fields, adopting comprehensive automation strategies, and fostering a culture of continuous experimentation and learning, organizations can confidently chart a course towards a future where their data infrastructure remains a powerful, efficient, and agile engine for driving innovation, extracting invaluable insights and achieving sustained success in the ever-expanding and increasingly complex Dataverse. The ongoing journey of managing and leveraging data is a continuous process of evolution, and the ability to adapt and embrace the unwritten future will be the ultimate key to long-term success in this dynamic and transformative landscape.

Architecting for the Petabyte Era concludes by underscoring that building robust, efficient, and future-proof data pipelines at petabyte scale is not merely a technical undertaking, but a strategic imperative for any organization seeking to thrive in the data-driven age. The journey from raw data to actionable insight in such vast quantities demands a holistic approach, encompassing thoughtful architectural design, strategic technology selection, rigorous security and governance frameworks, and a commitment to continuous optimization and adaptation. By embracing principles of parallelism, low latency processing where necessary, seamless interoperability, infrastructure-as-code, comprehensive automation, and proactive data governance with robust metadata management, organizations can transform the overwhelming challenge of petabyte-scale data into a powerful engine for innovation and competitive advantage. The ability to strategically navigate the temporal landscape of data processing, while diligently securing and responsibly governing this immense data ocean, ultimately defines a mature and agile data-driven enterprise, capable of unlocking the full potential of its data assets in a sustainable and trustworthy manner. The petabyte era presents both unprecedented opportunities and significant complexities, and mastering the art of architecting scalable data pipelines is the key to not just surviving but flourishing in this data-rich future.

www.ingramcontent.com/pod-product-compliance
Lightning Source LLC
Chambersburg PA
CBHW021432180326
41458CB00001B/234